Advance Praise

"David is a critical thinker, and his book gives real examples of how greater economic prosperity can provide the means for both stronger environmental stewardship and improving the human condition. Since I first met him over 30 years ago, David has been a globe-trekking economic optimist, and *The Facts of the Matter* is a must read for all of us interested in a real conversation moving forward."

—Arthur B. Laffer, father of Supply Side Economics and
economic policy advisor to President Reagan

"David Parish's proposition to utilize inquiry and engagement versus confrontation and advocacy is a great theme and powerful basis for the book. His plea for solutions over rhetoric and his invitation to others to come together for serious and fact-based discussion is the ultimate value of *The Facts of the Matter*. Parish is clearly on the side of making a difference versus creating a dust storm. I hope the book receives a wide circulation. We'd all be better off."

—John Hofmeister, former president of Shell Oil Company and author of
Why We Hate the Oil Companies: Straight Talk from an Energy Insider

"David captures what is possible when an 'all hands on deck' approach is applied to tackling our toughest challenges and the real possibilities for innovation that can happen when people with diverse views work together for the common good."

—General Joe Ralston, former Supreme Allied Commander, Europe, NATO
who led efforts to integrate 3 former Yugoslav states into NATO in 1999 and the
process to invite seven other former Communist nations to join NATO in 2002

"In *Facts of the Matter*, David Parish eschews the current trend toward overactive hyperbole, hyper-partisan politics, false equivalencies, and attacks on the fourth estate that keep political, business, and media leaders from legislating, implementing, and reporting fact- and data-driven solutions confronting contemporary society. Instead, Parish promotes reasoned thinking, civil dialog, and, most importantly, optimism while offering a broad array of counterintuitive resource, energy, environment, and policy solutions."

—Edward J. Ulman, chief executive officer and general manager, Alaska Public Media

"As a founder of the Alaska Federation of Natives and the author of the research report 'What Rights to Land Have the Alaska Natives: The Primary Issue,' I can say with absolute certainty that *The Facts of the Matter* is an excellent exploration of the nexus between resource development and environmental protection. He has cited our NANA experience and shown that resources can be developed and important subsistence and cultural values protected for the benefit of indigenous people as well as the state."

—William Hensley, founder of NANA Regional Corporation and Maniilaq, the regional nonprofit representing the tribes in the Kotzebue region; former president, executive director, and co-chairman of Alaska Federation of Natives; and author of *Fifty Miles from Tomorrow: A Memoir of Alaska and the Real People*

"More than most Americans, Alaskans struggle with the development vs environmental protection dilemma as we cherish our state's pristine beauty yet 'drill baby drill' for oil to maintain our affluence. Longtime natural resource lobbyist Dave Parish brings a fresh and readable perspective to that debate by tapping revealing examples of success and failure, from Belize and Russia to Madagascar and remote Alaska Native villages. Surprisingly for a guy who worked for Exxon and mining companies, Parish cites the likes of Barack Obama and Al Gore for thoughtful leadership. *The Facts of the Matter* forces you to rethink your biases as we all struggle to benefit a greater good.

—David Ramseur, author of *Melting the Ice Curtain: The Extraordinary Story of Citizen Diplomacy on the Russia-Alaska Frontier*

"Dave has long been a role model to me, showing how even the most controversial topics, such as resource development and climate change, can be discussed in a civil and rational manner, as *The Facts of the Matter* suggests. When warming winters clearly indicated the need for a snowmaking system in the Nordic skiing mecca of Anchorage, Alaska, Dave worked with us to bring olympic athletes, leaders in the environmental community, large oil and gas and mining companies, and others together to build world-class winter sports facilities that will benefit people for generations to come."

—Rachel Steer, US Biathlon champion and chief administrative officer at DOWL

LOOKING PAST TODAY'S RHETORIC

on the Environment *and* Responsible Development

The Facts of the Matter

DAVID PARISH

GREENLEAF
BOOK GROUP PRESS

This publication is designed to provide accurate and authoritative information in regard to the subject matter covered. This publication reflects the opinions of the author and all reasonable and good faith efforts have been undertaken to verify the veracity of all statements of opinion contained herein. This publication is made with the understanding that the publisher and author are not engaged in rendering legal, accounting, or other professional services. If legal advice or other expert assistance is required, the services of a competent professional should be sought.

Published by Greenleaf Book Group Press
Austin, Texas
www.gbgpress.com

Distributed by Greenleaf Book Group

For ordering information or special discounts for bulk purchases, please contact Greenleaf Book Group at PO Box 91869, Austin, TX 78709, 512.891.6100.

Design and composition by Greenleaf Book Group
Cover design by Greenleaf Book Group
Cover images: ©iStockphoto.com/hadynyah,
©iStockphoto.com/mattjeacock, ©iStockphoto.com/mrgao

Cataloging-in-Publication data is available.

Print ISBN: 978-1-62634-479-2

eBook ISBN: 978-1-62634-480-8

Part of the Tree Neutral® program, which offsets the number of trees consumed in the production and printing of this book by taking proactive steps, such as planting trees in direct proportion to the number of trees used: www.treeneutral.com

Printed in the United States of America on acid-free paper

18 19 20 21 22 23   10 9 8 7 6 5 4 3 2 1

First Edition

For my mom, Pat.

"For all our outward differences,
we're all in this together."

—President Barack Obama,
2017 farewell speech

Contents

Preface xi

1 Following the Herd toward the Cliff 1

2 So What Do We Do? 29

3 Yet There Is Hope! 35

4 How the Big Guy Can Help the Little Guys
Make an Even Bigger Difference 45

5 Raising Up Entire Societies 59

6 Increasing Wealth Can Increase Environmental Protection 71

7 Living a Collective Mentality of Abundance
Rather Than Scarcity 79

8 Think Differently 87

9 Improving How We Think and Teaching to Think 93

10 Improving the Environment through a Better
Society and Leadership 101

11 A New Path for Big Business 113

12 Improve Humanity 119

13 The Last Shall Be First 125

14 Better News Media 135

15 Better Political Leaders 147

16 A Better Future 157

Acknowledgments 175

Notes 177

About the Author 187

Preface

This book started five years ago as a rant about companies, politicians, media, government regulators, and interest groups taking advantage of our common desire to take care of the planet to sell us on bumper-sticker "green" products and policies that furthered their own agendas while often having the opposite effect of what they were packaged to do. Yet what resulted is a road map to address some of our most pressing issues on the need for strong environmental stewardship, the plague of childhood diarrhea deaths in poor countries, sex tourism, teen suicide, chronic obesity-related illnesses, developmental disabilities, and hunger.

Underlying all of this is a need for each and every one of us to be critical thinkers who question those selling us on oversimplified solutions to hard problems. I hope you will find this book thought provoking, be inspired to do your own research, and even question my suggested solutions along the way.

1

Following the Herd toward the Cliff

Two friends visiting over coffee at a local café a few years back were chatting about the latest green breakthrough that one of them had heard would stop global warming, save coastal cities from being washed away in the ensuing floods, clean the air, and save the planet. They were talking about a brand-new, ecologically revolutionary "eco-car" powered partially by an old-school gasoline-fired engine and partially by a battery that recharged as the car drove.

"In fact, now you can drive twice as far or more on just one tank of traditional gas and out-green your neighbors in the process!" said one. "And," he added, "the first consumers to buy these each year even get a federal tax break for saving the planet!"

His friend said, "Wow! Sounds too good to be true."

Just then, someone sitting at the next table leaned over and said, "Maybe it *is*."

Packaging their cars as "green," the world's biggest car makers are seeing huge profits with lines of "hybrids," with price premiums that are largely profit for them—straight to their bottom lines. They are particularly profitable for their parts and service departments, because hybrids require far more parts and equipment than traditional cars to support their dual gasoline and electric drive systems. Yet one of the biggest environmental ironies of the whole fad may be the battery-manufacturing process for these cars. Manufacture of the battery for the eco-car uses far more sophisticated metals than an old-school battery, and making the batteries is a highly energy-intensive process. The factories that make them are also virtually all on the traditional grid, powered largely by coal and fossil fuel.

The popularity of hybrid "eco-cars," despite a decidedly less "green" total footprint, is a classic example of the flaws in our current political, social, and cultural climates around the issue of environmentalism: We shun the nuance and complexities of these critical, world-changing issues in favor of bumper-sticker slogans and extreme positions. Mass hypocrisy and fearmongering have taken the place of critical thinking and reasoned dialogue. By oversimplifying and overlooking real problems, we too often preclude the possibility of real innovation and real solutions.

Shaping societal beliefs

A wave of "going green" is sweeping across the globe as caring for the planet has become a priority for many individuals and for most of society as a whole. It has taken on the significance of a spiritual experience for a great number of us, but as with many real and important human endeavors, the road to a precipitous cliff is paved with good intentions. We have a heartfelt desire to do the right thing for the planet, and as powerful interests take advantage of this, they play on our emotions and beliefs. In the process, our collective beliefs become even more skewed on the critical energy, resources, and environmental front.

Today's society has become conditioned by so many *save the last* campaigns, with their associated fear-based messaging, that we will do almost anything to save the planet, including buying virtually any product labeled as "green," because we think we are helping. And what I call *The Big Green Machine*—an informal and growing coalition of big media, big environmental groups, big government agencies, big businesses, and big politicians—knows this and plays to our emotions to advance their own agendas in the process. Underlying so many of these campaigns is a template, used over and over again, that inevitably creates perceptions of catastrophe. Along with that, we're constantly told that many of our day-to-day activities and actions are going to destroy the planet, hurt our kids, and end the world as we know it. These messages are in the news virtually every day, reshaping many societal beliefs in the process.

This leads to individual consumer and broader societal actions and decisions with regard to wise natural resource development, use, consumption, and conservation becoming increasingly skewed. When we hear something over and over again and believe it, it becomes our individual truth and, further, a societal truth. This reshaping of societal beliefs is especially harmful when it leads to collective beliefs based on fear rather than facts. New truths impact everything from individual consumer choices to national and global policies, often with huge environmental, economic, and social costs. They prevent us from making effective change, instead diverting our attention to shock value and only partial views of a story.

It is true that the planet's climate has been warming, glaciers have been receding around the world, and the polar ice cap has been melting for decades. However, the subtle and overt fear-based messaging that leads us to believe coastal cities like Manhattan face imminent threat of submersion is being used by various interests to further their own agendas, including those politicians who predicted the polar ice cap was going to completely melt in 2014.[1] Yes, the climate has been warming since the last ice age. And while the role of human activity and carbon emissions in global warming/climate change remains a hotly debated question, the fact is that many of the ideas we have been sold on as "solutions" actually lead to a larger environmental footprint around the globe.

The green machine

On a broad scale, environmental awareness has taken on many of the tenets of a traditional religious movement. A crusade dedicated to safeguarding the planet and its people, it has grown and morphed to include five major players: political leaders, government agencies, much of the media, advocacy groups, and big business. They are all part of an underlying movement that is playing to our individual spiritual connection to the planet and our desire to do the right thing. Yet if much of what we are being taught and told to do is not helping the planet and its people at all and, instead, may be doing just the opposite, how are so many people falling for it?

Much of the latest wave of "going green" began in the mid- and late-1980s, as environmental activist groups struggled to maintain their relevance. The global economy was growing at an increasing rate, and new environmental laws and technological breakthroughs were cleaning up the air and water across the United States and other developed countries. That wave changed direction on March 24, 1989, a day that will live on in infamy, as the *Exxon Valdez* ran aground—unleashing the largest oil spill in American history. I was a newly hired Exxon public affairs person thrust into the national spotlight as one of their primary international spokesmen in Valdez (the Alaskan port the vessel was named after) at the time of the disaster. I saw firsthand how politicians, government, the media, environmental groups, and even the company itself handled this disaster differently in a world transitioning toward 24-hour news cycles and increasingly sophisticated messaging.

There were many very sincere, intellectually honest, and well-intentioned members of the news media, government officials, environmental activists, and company people engaged at the time; however, any voices of reason were too often drowned out by the loudest and most emotional ones. Those loud voices were the ones caught by the TV cameras, a trend that has become far too prevalent on too many environmental and natural resource issues today.

Objective science and environmental collaboration were one of the most tragic losers in what became the largest corporate public relations disaster of our time. Just as the hybrid car dichotomy illustrates the problem with environmentalism in a microcosm, the *Exxon Valdez* spill perfectly illustrates the power players propagating the myth of modern environmentalism.

CULPRIT #1: BIG MEDIA

Somewhere along the way, many of us got the impression that the news media followed a certain set of common journalistic ethical practices. We came to believe that reporters, especially those with big, credible, statewide, national, and international media outlets, had all been taught and adhered to a set of standards, including things like remaining impartial, covering all sides of a story, and fact-checking sources and information in the process. We believed that reporters had editors overseeing their work. Above the editors, we further believed, were publishers who did the same.

My own experience as a primary worldwide spokesman for Exxon during the first days of the *Exxon Valdez* oil spill crisis in Alaska confirmed how those beliefs were put into practice by media of that era. My role in the first days of the crisis involved contact with media from all over the world, both by phone and in person with those who descended into Valdez in the days after the spill. During that time, I interacted regularly with one of the world's leading old-school traditional journalists of that era, senior *Washington Post* correspondent Jay Mathews, who was on the scene in Valdez.

Mathews, who is still a senior columnist with *The Post*, tracked me down in person, a spokesman for a company under global fire in the heat of the worst global environmental and public relations disaster of our time, in the small hotel serving as makeshift command center, and handed me a roll of foil paper that looked like a long grocery store receipt. He produced it from some sort of early portable printer. It was a copy of the story he was about to file that night for the next morning's edition of *The Washington Post*, four time zones away. It was a story guaranteed to run on the front page the next morning, and his request was that I fact-check everything that related to the company—all of its quotes and the facts and figures about the spill that had come from company statements.

Mathews was confident in the story angles he had already chosen. He was independent and clearly could not be swayed in that independence by the growing army of fisherman, environmentalists, state regulators, company people, or anyone else who was out pushing their own angle on what had become the biggest environmental story of our generation. Mathews was confident enough in his own objectivity and committed enough to get all of his facts right that he would share the draft story with me, and possibly people from the other interests involved, to verify the factual accuracy of what he was reporting.

Unfortunately, reporters like Mathews now find themselves in the minority in most newsrooms. News media staffs and budgets have been cut dramatically in the reshaping of the big media industry in the digital age. Many big news organizations are down to a third or a quarter of the staffs they had as recently as the mid-1990s. Correspondingly, these cutbacks coincide with an age of advocacy journalism, where a new generation of reporters, editors, and publishers are increasingly out to advance specific political, economic, social, and environmental agendas through their big media outlets and conglomerates.

In the evolving new age of "journalism" of the past 20-plus years, this trend has been most profound in coverage of environmental issues. In the environmental and natural resource policy arena, media increasingly choose story angles focusing on environmental controversy, worst-case scenarios, sensational headlines, Armageddon-hype angles, and "big business is bad" messaging. We've all seen the headlines: "Warming report sees sicker, poorer future" (Associated Press, November 3, 2013) to "Climate change threatens coffee, chocolate" (*Tribune* Washington Bureau, May 13, 2013), as well as "With more ships in the Arctic, fears of disaster rise" (*New York Times*, July 23, 2017).

On climate change issues, reporters often go to the same pro- and anti-climate change "experts" for quotes to fill in the blanks in reaction to these new "expert" reports. While reporters write the stories that reshape our societal beliefs, editors skew the headlines toward extreme, sensational angles designed to get readers' and viewers' attention and hook them in, thus increasing media ratings and, subsequently, media sales. When reporters increasingly go back to the same "sources" again and again, knowing who they can call who will be opinionated and quotable—and, often, what these sources will say before they say it—is fill-in-the-blank reporting. And the more we hear them, the more we believe their perspectives are fact rather than one-sided opinion.

CULPRIT #2: ENVIRONMENTAL ADVOCACY GROUPS

The problem of oversimplifying in our sound-byte culture goes far beyond the media. Too often today, big global, professional environmental organizations increasingly take a far more simplistic approach, appealing to our emotions, using bumper-sticker slogans and rhetoric to incite emotion and fear over science to advance their causes.

Back in the 1960s and 1970s, the sincere basic tenets of the modern environmental movement were founded on a desire for truth and greater environmental protections based on scientific facts, as a lack of scientific environmental and regulatory oversight was an underlying factor in our nation's air and water pollution. A movement grew advocating for much-needed stronger environmental protections based on science, and the need for stronger formal processes for environmental permitting, with higher bars. The movement advocated for formal, scientific processes to decide major natural resource policy decisions and supported the enactment of the National Environmental Policy Act, the Clean Water Act, the Clean Air Act, and the Endangered Species Act. This led to a quantum shift in societal decision-making. The combination of modern science, technology, and these laws, along with the standards and processes they established, helped clean up our air and water across the country.

When I started college in Los Angeles in 1982, the Clean Air Act and associated standards, such as the phase-out of leaded gasoline, were still transitioning into effect. At the time, there were rarely days you could see from the mountains to the sea across the basin due to the famous smog and poor air quality that had come to define Los Angeles itself. When my own daughter started college in Los Angeles 30 years later, my visits to the new Los Angeles of the 21st century revealed a far different situation than when I had been a student there just a few decades earlier. Now, it is a rare day when you *cannot* see from the base of the San Gabriel Mountains in Pasadena to the sea across the Los Angeles Basin. This is truly one of the greatest environmental cleanup stories of our generation. Yet it isn't anything we see cited in professional environmental group newsletters or on bumper stickers. Why not?

Like the media, advocacy groups too often ignore the good in favor of the outrageous—and ignore the complexities in favor of oversimplified single-issue stances. Take another example: In my home state of Alaska, media have inundated us in recent years with headlines about studies warning that global warming is melting the polar ice cap and could threaten the very existence of iconic polar bears, one of the most interesting, hearty, intelligent, and fascinating creatures in the Arctic. Armed with these studies, advocacy groups petitioned the US government to put polar bears on the US Fish and Wildlife Service's endangered species list in 2008, initiating a process that, if successful, would result in wide-ranging federal restrictions on human activity across the US Arctic. It all sounded straightforward enough, and the issue gained international momentum as well-meaning people across the globe heard the doomsday headlines and started stampeding to "save" the polar bears.

Yet some people reacted in a surprisingly different way, as key Alaska Iñupiat Eskimo Native leaders stepped into the debate. These leaders were focused on both caring for the natural Arctic environment that is so critical to their subsistence hunting and fishing culture and improving the socioeconomic plight of Alaska Natives living in the Arctic, people who are often still relegated to living in challenging conditions. These Native leaders asked about finding a balance between the impacts of the proposed restrictions on their human activity, which is necessary for the pursuit of much-needed economic opportunity for the

Iñupiat Eskimo people. The proposed restrictions could preclude this opportunity, thus hindering Iñupiat efforts toward self-determination, economic self-sufficiency, and the associated improvements in basic public health, high-quality education, and affordable housing and energy for their people. Many of us in the developed urban world take these necessities for granted, but too often they are in desperate short supply among many Native people living in the Arctic.

As the global media converged on the story, highlighting the angle that human activity in the Arctic must be stopped in order to save the polar bears from global warming, the associated messages incited emotions and worst-case scenarios, motivating people from faraway places across the globe to start signing online petitions supporting the restrictions. Yet along the way, how many who heard these predictions of doom asked probing questions about the underlying science that was spooking the societal herd to stampede, and how many asked how that stampede would impact the rights and future lives of Alaska Natives living in the Arctic?

The future of polar bears is just one example of how the global debate on environmental and resource development and use decisions is increasingly based on advocacy science. This brand of science is put forward by those with specific agendas. Society tends to believe "experts," whether they are objective or not. And too often, most of us don't question objectivity and agendas enough, especially as interests hire more and more scientists and "experts" to support their agendas and predrawn conclusions.

As a part of the emotion-based calls to action, professional organizations are continually calling on us to act to save the last _____ from impending destruction. Yet, while the Endangered Species Act and the litany of other environmental laws of the 1970s were important in turning the tide of protecting the environment and species under severe threat, how many more *save the last*s do we need?

CULPRIT #3: GOVERNMENT AGENCIES

Big government agencies also reshape beliefs through their choice of words and the use of a sophisticated press release machinery to get their messages out. The EPA (Environmental Protection Agency), along with too many other federal, state, and local environmental regulatory agencies, uses the same sophisticated messaging, psychology, and word choices as the news media and professional environmental groups. Agencies that are supposed to be rooted in science, fact, and process have become a part of the oversimplified, fear-based, bumper-sticker messaging. These big government agencies employ their own internal PR people to craft and polish messaging and write press releases to ensure they are quotable. This strategy is particularly pronounced on environmental and natural resource policy issues, with the EPA at the forefront. Created in the 1970s in concert with the National Environmental Policy Act and the other environmental laws of the time, the EPA's charge was to bring modern science- and technology-based solutions and standards to ensure protection of the environment and maintain the quality of our air and water.

So why would an agency with that mandate ever need to hire professional PR people to craft press releases and create a spin machine that grinds out more press releases than most businesses? In fact, the EPA has even had its own Newsroom website, putting out as many as 10–20 press releases every single day, more than all of the Big Oil companies combined! These press releases use specific fear-based messaging to emphasize negative aspects of stories, to shame, and to scapegoat:

- "Kotzebue, Alaska, is the most toxic city in the U.S. thanks to Red Dog mine pollution" (February 18, 2018)

- "Under settlement, North Windham, Conn., company reduces hazardous waste" (April 20, 2015)

- "EPA: Boise-based ski and snowboard park developer required to properly clean up asbestos to protect workers and area residents" (April 13, 2015)

- "Stamford, Conn., property management firm to pay fine and take measures to protect children from lead-based paint in EPA settlement" (April 15, 2015)

- "Major egg producer to reduce water pollution discharges at Mississippi facility" (April 13, 2015)

- "Mercury incident at Yakima home requires EPA emergency cleanup" (April 16, 2015)

At the same time, the EPA issued an even larger daily barrage of press releases lauding and reinforcing what the agency views as lofty social behavior, including free advertising for hybrid cars. In today's world, too many government agencies operate press release and public education machines relentlessly, impacting societal thinking in the process. Whether to justify their budgets or simply educate us, this government agency approach makes things worse, polarizes us, reshapes beliefs, and, too often, ultimately harms the environment, the economy, and our planet.

CULPRIT #4: BIG BUSINESS

In sometimes subtle and other times overt ways, many businesses brand themselves and their products to fit societal beliefs and "truths." In doing so, they often perpetuate those beliefs themselves, regardless of whether the beliefs are correct, based on factual data, or based on emotion. This is especially true around current societal fears about the environment and impending destruction of our planet.

Buying a hybrid for many is, unfortunately, based more on emotion and the consumer feeling good and being proud of his or her "green" vehicle than on accurate facts about how to minimize the human footprint on our planet. Even the initial economic arguments about hybrids' high gas mileage often don't pencil, as human innovation, technical breakthroughs, and the use of high-strength lightweight metals and plastics have driven up the mileage efficiency of standard cars dramatically. And now, fully electric cars are proliferating at an accelerating rate, even bucking the hybrid fad, as old-school car manufacturers around the globe are making real, meaningful environmental improvements.

Hybrids are status symbols for many environmentally conscious consumers, profit generators for those who make them and their service and parts departments, and political darlings of politicians and the media—all despite the fact that many of these "green" products often have a far bigger carbon footprint than traditional alternatives, requiring far more metals and energy to produce than a standard car, with more and more of the raw materials coming from places with far laxer environmental standards than we have here in the United States. But hybrids are just one example of a wide-scale problem in the consumer market. Green marketing affects companies from Coca-Cola to Apple and leads to the same problem: While answering our hunger for "green" products, they often obscure the answers to the questions we really should be asking: Is this product really making the difference it says it's making? And more importantly, where, exactly, are these products coming from?

It is increasingly common for mega–big businesses to position themselves and their products as environmental saviors. Apple is just one of the latest big businesses to jump on the bandwagon as their sophisticated PR spin machine tries to deflect attention from the global "sucking sound" that is coming from the products they manufacture. In regard to their energy usage footprint, Apple's own corporate website says the following:

Constantly finding new ways to conserve natural resources and use less energy is a crucial part of our manufacturing process. We're partnering with suppliers to generate and procure more than 4 gigawatts of new clean power worldwide by 2020 to reduce emissions from manufacturing. In 2018, all of our suppliers are required to set carbon reduction goals. We also created a Clean Water Program that encourages factories to find ways to conserve fresh water and reuse wastewater. As a result, participating factories in China have achieved an average reuse rate of 37 percent, exceeding the industry average of 30 percent.[2]

Apple's pitch sounds good and is obviously designed to make us all feel better about buying more of their sleek, new, subtly green-marketed products—but how many of us ask where these 4 gigawatts of new "clean" power will come from? And how many of us ask Apple whether the metals and petroleum products used to make the servers and equipment in their data centers magically come from outer space or are mined and produced in the United States versus third- and fourth-world countries? And where do the materials for the new facilities that reduce wastewater in China come from?

In the rush to green everything from soda cans to fossil fuels, we throw out the possibility of making real change. Society ultimately loses a great deal of productivity as technologies that truly are more environmentally sound are sacrificed for the sake of businesses trying to satisfy our growing appetite for bumper-sticker solutions to environmental problems.

CULPRIT #5: POLITICIANS

Having spent the past 30-plus years working closely with politicians of all political persuasions, my experience is that the vast majority of our elected officials are conscientious, hardworking, ethical people who truly want to make a difference. And my own experience is that no political party has a monopoly on being right, including on environmental issues. Politicians of each party have leanings toward solutions for issues and tendencies to support certain causes or do things in certain ways. But there is often more consensus than not.

Yet one thing that leading politicians of both major parties do in today's competitive world of extremes is make increasingly aggressive and radical statements to get quoted in the press. Getting quoted means more free name recognition. A form of free advertising, it means more exposure, which helps them gain power. When politicians make extreme statements, it makes it harder to distinguish whether they are really trying to make the world a better place or just trying to advance their agendas. Marketing experts say that the more a name is quoted or a statement is heard, the more it sticks in people's memories. This creates a dangerous cycle with modern-day journalists intent on feeding their ratings machines rather than finding the center of the story. Because the more radical statements are the ones that the media picks up and quotes, the more those statements are heard over and over again, and the more they are believed. The more they are believed, the more people are motivated to act—the dangerous cycle continues. Saying things like "Everything will be fine; we are working together to find common solutions to complicated problems" won't get them quoted nearly as much as extreme statements that stand out. And nowhere is this more pronounced than on environmental and natural resource policy issues.

As Sarah Palin demonstrated, *Drill, baby, drill!* certainly makes for a quotable statement that fits on a bumper sticker. Yet it grossly oversimplifies complicated energy issues—even for those of us who support increased oil and gas development in the United States—just as blaming those same oil companies for global warming and the impending destruction of our planet oversimplifies important issues. The Keystone Pipeline is a classic case of the way discussion of viable alternatives and associated net impacts has been pushed to the side by the informal conspiracy of bumper-sticker rhetoric playing to the herd. As more and more worst-case scenarios and arguments against the project were raised by the sophisticated coalition fighting it, the total net impact of not building the project was rarely discussed. We heard little about not only the import of more crude oil from third-world sources with lower environmental and human rights standards than Canada but also the impact of Canada sending this energy to its own West Coast instead, for export to Asia—much of it to China.

Where were *The New York Times*, the BBC, and other global news media that have given so much attention to China's environmental problems and exponentially growing carbon emissions when it came to questioning the professionals organizing the Keystone opposition on the impact of sending this crude oil to China instead, a jurisdiction cited by many as one of the largest sources of Arctic haze and the potential link associated with the acceleration of global warming? Yet Keystone opponents, Obama cabinet officials, the EPA and other federal agencies, news media columnists, and environmentalists rarely challenged us to consider these bigger questions. Keystone became a classic case of informal conspiracies inciting the herd to stop this individual project without considering the comprehensive, global impact of the alternatives. All of these players failed to take a global view and ask the really hard questions.

Policy decisions based on political expediency are too often making things worse for the planet because independent, objective facts and science are too often not sought—or are outright ignored—by our political leaders. As our current political system leads to increasingly divisive and convoluted decision-making, it begs the questions: Who is in charge, and what is their real agenda?

We should never underestimate human ingenuity and how quickly it can flow, along with investment capital, to find innovative technological breakthroughs that benefit the planet and people. Today, we need political leaders who will support and encourage this more than ever. Unfortunately, right now, extremism from politicians on both ends of the spectrum is chasing that ingenuity out of the United States and Canada in droves. In the process, energy investment is flowing to places like Russia and the Middle East, and mining investment is flowing to places with laxer environmental protections than we have right here.

THE BOTTOM LINE

These players aren't all getting in a room together and conspiring, but they are all doing the same thing. They all have legitimate concern for the environment, but the societal tragedy is that, because so many look out for number one, the environment is not getting better when they incite the herds. In reality, the stampedes they so often trigger can make things worse for the environment and the economy, as reasonable voices on complicated issues are trampled by the herd, who are instigated by bumper-sticker rhetoric.

The facts of the matter

There are fewer and fewer impartial referees in today's political and cultural climate, and the 50-yard line is increasingly dominated by shouting matches rather than handshakes. As President Obama said in his 2017 farewell address to the nation, "Without some common baseline of facts, without a willingness to admit new information and concede that your opponent might be making a fair point and that science and reason matter, then we're going to keep talking past each other." Ultimately, biased input leads to biased output.

These big players in today's environmental movement can all be charged with the same thing: obscuring complex truths with bumper-sticker rhetoric designed to incite fear or sell products (or people). The fact of the matter? This may actually be accelerating impacts on the planet elsewhere, in short order. As we take so much time, energy, and money to protect our own backyards, we are exporting our production to other parts of the world—out of our own yards, out of sight, out of mind. But we are still very much affecting the global environment in the process. Herein lies the danger.

EXPORTING PRODUCTION

A classic example of this is an ironic story related to two proposed mines in the United States, both located in southeast Alaska. One could help put a dent in China's 90-plus percent control of global rare earth metals production, and the other could produce the copper that goes into so many of our gadgets, recreational equipment, and hybrid cars. Both projects were based on designs with the strictest modern environmental practices and technologies. As I sat in a crowded hearing room behind the lobbyist for an environmental group who was about to testify against these projects, I noticed he was busily typing away on a sleek, modern smartphone and taking pictures of committee documents and handouts on that same phone to email to people in his network across the globe over the fossil fuel–based Internet.

The irony of this was lost on many in the room but not on one of the lawmakers, who asked after his testimony if this advocacy group was opposed to these mines to produce the metals for smartphones like the one the lobbyist carried that day, then where should the materials for these things come from? The lobbyist reacted like a deer in the headlights, offering no answer on where the stuff for his stuff should come from. Isn't it time that we all go deeper in this conversation? We should insist on answers to the question "If not here, then where?"

Our society's exponentially increasing use of electronic devices is staggering. As we plug in our ever-growing collections of electronics, refrigerators, and now even cars to charge overnight in our homes, global demand for copper, nickel, cerium, and many other rare earth metals grows. Our total energy footprint per person is increasing with all of these gadgets. While they may be packaged to look clean, sleek, and green, the reality is that their production and use is sucking up energy at an exponential rate.

The average American household contains over 25 consumer electronic devices, according to a US Department of Energy article.[3] As our Apple and Samsung phones and tablets become more and more powerful, they also demand more and more power to run and more and more metals for their manufacture. These devices are one of the reasons the growing electronic economy uses so much electricity. They are based increasingly on the power-sucking server farms that make up the backbone of the Internet and the cloud. As reported in *Time* magazine, "Our computers and smartphones might seem clean, but the digital economy uses a tenth of the world's electricity—and that share will only increase, with serious consequences for the economy and the environment."[4] The report *Time* based its story on estimated that this electronic economy now uses 1,500 terawatt-hours of power per year. That's about 10 percent of the world's total electricity generation—the same as the combined power production of Germany and Japan and the same amount of electricity that was used to light the entire planet as recently as 1985! And where will all of that electricity come from?

Virtually every single component in these things comes from mining or oil and gas production. And yet, in today's system, obtaining the permits and approvals needed to build a mine in the United States takes an average of seven years, among the longest wait times in the world.[5] We now have a decision process driven by those in the supercities that makes it increasingly hard to produce raw materials in the rest of the country to fill this growing demand. This dichotomy results in the export of more and more of our manufacturing and production overseas—out of sight, out of mind.

Increasing demand for copper, molybdenum, zinc, rare earths, and other metals leads inexorably to more mineral and energy production. This cycle spurs accelerating global demand for mining and oil and gas production, increasing pressure to produce more and produce it faster, which can lead to more and more production in jurisdictions that may have less rigorous environmental standards, places where they can be produced more quickly and often at a lower cost than in our own backyards.

WHOSE BACKYARD?

The one-lane main north–south highway through the huge African island country of Madagascar is famous for its potholes and slow, treacherous driving conditions. The highway is traveled mainly by 15-passenger Mazda vans converted to *taxi-brousses*, always packed with seemingly twice that many people, along with luggage and people and chickens clinging to the cargo racks on top. When I traveled this route in 2013, I saw hordes of people walking along the sides of the road—women walking barefoot in brightly colored traditional African dresses, many carrying babies in front and backpacks. Barefoot toddlers often followed behind, and men on bicycles rode back and forth between settlements in the grassland and jungle, carrying bushels of bananas and chickens to trade. In this fourth-world place, a staggering number of people live in thatched-roof huts with palm leaf siding, no electricity, and no running water or sewer.

Along the side of the road one morning, I saw young Malagasy kids, most of them looked about kindergarten age, waving at the vans and trucks going by, begging for money for the gravel they had filled into some of the endless sea of the potholes along the road.

On the other side of the highway was a sight I will never forget. Large families with wooden makeshift hammers pounded away at piles of rocks in front of their huts. Adult men, women, young children, and old people were all crouched over in the rapidly heating up late-morning sun.

I asked our driver what they were doing, and he said, "Making cement."

"What?"

"Yes, making cement."

He explained that these poor families regularly go into the nearby hills and pull out limestone themselves or barter for chunks of it from nearby subsistence miners. Then they spend countless days, weeks, and months crouched in front of their huts, breaking the stone into smaller pieces that can then be sold to cement makers in the poor, isolated country. All of this still happened in 2013, where I could take pictures of their huts and stone piles with either of the two modern camera smartphones I was carrying, both made entirely of mining and petroleum products that often come from unknown third- and fourth-world sources in the complicated, modern, global supply chain.

As political efforts stop more and more projects here in our own backyards in response to *save the last* campaigns, production is forced elsewhere. As a result, more and more of us are increasingly disconnected from where the stuff for our stuff comes from. That often means exporting that production to third- and fourth-world places like Madagascar, with child labor that I saw firsthand as those young kids worked from sunrise to sunset breaking rocks with their bare hands, with little medical care and even less hope of ever attending school.

ASKING THE TOUGH QUESTIONS

The growing groupthink herd mentality motivates people, governments, and businesses to take actions and make decisions that can lead to the exact opposite result of what they are trying to accomplish. Along the way, this societal collective attack on common sense and reason leads to decisions based on emotion rather than fact, often making things worse for human society and the planet in the process. Why don't more of us stand up and ask tough questions?

North America continues to lead the world in many technological breakthroughs, human ingenuity, and creativity, often in spite of our political leaders, media, and activist movements. We've driven breakthroughs in research and development, technology, environmental sciences, applied technology, nanotechnology, and biotechnology. So, with this creative ingenuity, can we also apply the latest technologies to the use of natural resources necessary for our supercities and associated modern amenities? And can we do this within a regulatory process based on the highest scientific standards in the world, with fact- and science-based decision-making systems like the National Environmental Policy Act, the Clean Water Act, and the Clean Air Act? Can we apply this technology and innovation to projects right here in North America, through the same sorts of modern technology that is necessary for "sustainable" cities, gardens, and farms?

We should apply these same principles to mineral and energy development, all with oversight from regulatory agencies under processes applying modern technology and science, with tested reliable building standards and practices. Surely, we can have the strongest environmental stewardship in the world, do things right, and be a case study in human development and environmental stewardship. And if we can do that here, can those same standards of excellence be applied to the developing world?

Can we lift up environmental stewardship in third- and fourth-world countries? What if we can improve environmental stewardship *and* economies in the third- and fourth-world at the same time?

Environmental groups, media, politicians, big government agencies, and big businesses don't get together in a room and conspire to mislead society, but they are part of the groupthink mentality that all too often leads society off the cliff. Time may be running out for society and the planet, and the responsibility is ours to stand up and change this, not theirs. We collectively need to stop letting politicians, the news media, big government agencies, big environmental groups, and big business spoon-feed us the answers we want to hear. We need to start asking more critical questions, thinking for ourselves, and holding them accountable to the truth, even when it is hard and inconvenient for us to hear.

In asking these questions, pushing back, and uncovering the truth, we need to be critical thinkers ourselves. Just as we shine light on them, when we flip on our own light switch, we need to understand that the electricity doesn't come from that switch but from a global power grid where electrons are transmitted to our iDevices and electric car plug-ins through copper wires. And we need to remind our kids, friends, and community of that. When we buy milk at the store, we need to remind ourselves and others that the milk doesn't come from a carton but from a cow and is transported to us through a sophisticated modern transportation system based almost entirely on fossil fuel energy and vehicles made of mined products. When that same grocery store hypes its "recycled" plastic and paper bags, rather than feeling better about using more bags and patting that big business on the back, we need to ask big grocery store chains what the total environmental, energy, and carbon footprint is from their promotion and use of recycled bags.

As politicians, big regulators, environmental groups, and others band together to oppose new power generation or transmission projects, we all need to push them with hard questions, including what they propose as viable alternatives. When big businesses pitch us on quick-fix products and policies, we need to question that. And we need to push the media, politicians, and governments to do the same.

When auto makers, battery manufacturers, environmental groups, and the EPA put a societal "green" stamp on hybrids, we need to question their motivations, their facts, and their logic.

We need to understand the facts of the matter and not just the rhetoric.

A CHANGE IN PERSPECTIVE

After I saw the child laborers making cement with their bare hands during my trip to Madagascar, our bus ride stopped for lunch at a small, local makeshift café deep in the jungle. We were the only customers at the roadside stop, a spot with a few plastic tables and chairs on one side and, on the other side of a palm leaf wall, a local artisan jewelry display area. The proprietor was a European-educated Malagasy man who said his vision for the shop was to allow local jewelry makers to connect directly with tourists, allowing the artisans to share in more of the economic return from their work. The jewelry included various types of colorful stones, and behind the tables on the wall was a map entitled "Madagascar and Its Mines" in French, showing where all of the stones in the jewelry had come from, along with a cute image of a rare Lemur.

Author Photo

When I asked him what his view of mining was, his answer surprised me.

"It's our country's hope for the future," he said.

This was not the answer I expected, as my life experience was that posters about mining that included cute wildlife pictures more typically came from activist groups, with associated messages to save creatures like the last baby lemur, political calls to action to stop projects, or pitches to send money to save the planet.

I pressed him. "Why do you say that?"

He said that a "big" outside company called Rio Tinto was developing a large-scale modern mine in southern Madagascar, several hundred kilometers away, using modern science and creating economic opportunity of unprecedented proportions in the fourth-world country. This economic opportunity reached all the way to his region, in the northern end of the country, several hundred kilometers away, as it was the site of Madagascar's primary deepwater port. Activity related to the mine necessitated huge volumes of material coming through the port, which would create jobs, including for the truck drivers who stopped to eat and resupply as they went through his region.

So rather than the rape-and-pillage images that media and societal herd beliefs have portrayed about the "natural resource curse" that mining and energy development supposedly bring to third- and fourth-world countries, here was a local entrepreneur seeing the glass as half full rather than half empty. And this was coming at a time when many people back home in the "developed world" had puzzled looks on their faces when I told them about my experiences in a "fourth-world" country, because they had never heard that term and had no idea that there is an economic status lower than third world. These are places where something beyond handouts and subsidies from abroad are necessary to provide the sustainable means to lift them up—places where millions of people are living below even third-world conditions.

Responsible companies and governments acting on true science and facts rather than emotions may be showing all of us a path forward toward a new global approach based on abundance rather than scarcity. Much of this comes through human ingenuity and creativity, spurred by optimistic thinking from some surprising sources. It would do the world a great deal of good if we all shifted our perspectives to the glass-half-full approach of this Malagasy entrepreneur.

It's so easy to get caught up in this current frenzy of "going green." But as a society and as people, we need to take a more discerning approach to the way we do that. Just because you buy a hybrid car doesn't mean you're doing your part (and you might even be doing more harm than good). We must stop putting so much power in the hands of big media, big environmental groups, big government agencies, big businesses, and big politicians. They have their own agendas in mind, whether it's intentional or not. We must go deeper and move away from bumper-sticker mentality. Our future depends on it.

2

So What Do We Do?

More than ten years ago, the 100,000-person-strong global mining giant Anglo American came to Alaska to evaluate the company's potential participation in a controversial mine project I had been working on for several years. Anglo is a South African–based, London-headquartered European company, on the leading edge of progressive, multinational mining initiatives. They are committed to forward-looking collective engagement on environmental, public health, and sustainability issues, leading change in an industry I have worked in and around for years.

When Anglo's people came to Alaska doing due diligence to assess the controversial project firsthand, they started by having me set up a meeting with Alaska's then-governor, Sarah Palin. Palin, at the time, was pushing through huge tax increases on Alaska's largest businesses (the energy industry) in order to finance the dramatic growth in government that Alaska experienced during her reign.

The notorious fog in Alaska's capital city of Juneau forced the plane carrying the two Anglo people to overshoot Juneau and land at the remote coastal village of Yakutat, which is physically cut off from the rest of the world, accessible only by air once per day. When they got off the plane and went into the small, one-room airport terminal, the European executives immediately felt out of place in their finest London suits and ties and faced another problem: They hadn't eaten in hours, hadn't had time during their 24-hour journey from London to get any American dollars, and found that there was no place to eat at the Yakutat airport. The only vending machine in the remote airport did not take credit cards, much less British pounds or euros—just old-fashioned US $1 bills and coins. A local saw their predicament and bought them each a bag of potato chips from the vending machine—*crisps* as they called them—welcomed them to Alaska, and wished them well on their journey.

When I finally caught up with them the next day in Anchorage, I discovered that although they didn't carry US cash when they traveled, they did keep track of their individual carbon footprint, one of them even paying an extra surcharge on his ticket from London for something called *carbon credits*. This surcharge cost more than his bag of "crisps" at the Yakutat airport.

Carbon credits is still largely a term as foreign as *crisps* to most Americans. Keeping track of one's individual environmental footprint was core to how the people from this company operated and how they approached doing the right thing for the planet. The company and project team later designed what would have been a leading-edge mine in a remote part of Alaska, with a significant portion of its power generated by renewable wind, also out of a desire to do the right thing for the planet. The project even put forward public plans to help bring affordable power from the potential mine to villages in the remote region that currently relied on some of the world's most expensive fossil fuel for their heat and electricity. Yet those efforts went largely ignored by many Alaskans who got caught up in the controversial rhetoric around the project, much of it a classic case of the all-or-nothing, black-and-white environment of the current US political system. As I later explained to these two Europeans at dinner one night, to Alaskans, "cap and trade" is something you do to a moose after a successful hunt, not anything related to global energy policy.

Anglo's continuing commitment to do the right thing for the planet at corporate and individual levels was rarely acknowledged or understood by many involved in the debate about the potential mine project. This was especially true among professional activist groups.

During this time, I received a donor solicitation piece in the mail from one of the international environmental groups opposing the project. It encouraged people to donate to their cause in order to save the planet, and those who gave more than a certain amount of money would be rewarded with a reusable, branded grocery shopping bag. This solicitation was targeted at well-meaning people. Yet the vast majority of those giving their financial support had no idea what sorts of campaigns the multinational group was undertaking with their donations; they just wanted to do the right thing and donate to making the world a better place. This included participation in a sophisticated campaign to oppose the mine designed by Anglo people with a similar desire to do the right thing for the planet. This company, whose senior executives put tracking their individual carbon footprints ahead of carrying money to eat when they traveled, wanted to design a state-of-the-art mine in Alaska based on the best modern science and technology, potentially largely powered by renewable energy sources, just like Apple's plant in Prineville, Oregon, but on a much larger scale. Yet the increasingly dysfunctional US political system, combined with other market factors, eventually caused Anglo to pull out of the project.

So what do we do as a society when activist groups tug at our heartstrings and appeal to our emotions for our money and then use those dollars on campaigns that often have the effect of exporting mineral and energy development necessary for the most basic human living to third- and fourth-world places like the Congo with far too high a prevalence of child labor and often lesser standards for environmental stewardship?

We live in a time when people are yearning for answers more than ever before on questions of how we save the planet from perceived inevitable environmental destruction, climate change, and population explosion. The dramatic popularity of movies like *An Inconvenient Truth* shows the societal desire to do the right thing and be responsible environmental stewards at a personal, local, and global level. The growing number of successful "green" products demonstrates people's well-intentioned concern for the planet, often without regard to where even the materials for these "green" products come from in the first place. So how do we harness this energy and use it productively for societal good? How do we turn this around and move away from bumper-sticker mentalities that make people feel good about buying into "green" products and causes while often having the opposite effect?

Think logically; act globally

All of this energy can be harnessed and redirected in ways to accomplish incredible environmental and societal good. There are things we can all do, starting with the need to stop falling prey to extremist agendas from people, politicians, media, big businesses, and those who aren't really helping but, instead, hurt the cause for their own benefit. When groups solicit our donations or companies sell us on their "green" products, we can look to multiple data sources, not just their respective bumper stickers. We can take thoughtful positions based on facts and data, not just react to sophisticated messaging that is designed to tug at our heartstrings. We can talk to others, including those with different perspectives and different beliefs from our own, and avoid what I call *cul-de-sac thinking* and what former president Obama calls a situation where "increasingly, we become so secure in our bubbles that we start accepting only information, whether it's true or not, that fits our opinions, instead of basing our opinions on the evidence that is out there." Obama was referring to the sort of groupthink that *Watchman's Rattle* author Rebecca Costa says stifles the diversity of views on complicated issues that have been critical to the survival of human civilizations for millennia—with numerous examples, from the Mayans to the Romans and the Nazis, having disintegrated largely due to follow-the-herd groupthink while stifling diversity of views from those outside their bubbles.

We can demand the same from our elected officials, regulators, and news media. Along the way, we can make things better for people all across the globe and become better environmental stewards in the process.

We can view the glass as half full rather than half empty.

3

Yet There Is Hope!

Educational opportunity was the message from Bill Gates, speaking to us in 2005 at the National Conference of State Legislatures (NCSL) in Seattle, ahead of ExxonMobil's chief economist presenting their long-term projections for economic growth and energy usage in each region across the globe. Most striking were the ExxonMobil economist's projections for population and economic growth in Latin America and the Asia-Pacific regions, areas filled with seemingly insurmountable social strife, civil wars, economic stagnation, and abject poverty not so many years before. It was fascinating to see countries like Mexico and China, who had been economic laggards for the past hundred years, predicted to be economic growth engines in the 21st century.

This was later borne out, as the World Economic Forum in 2015 said that Mexico's $1.26 trillion economy made it the 15th largest in the world, the country a sharply rising "economic power to be reckoned with."

When the 2005 conference was held, amid growing political paralysis and challenges throughout the United States and a proliferation of the glass-half-empty viewpoint, I was working for ExxonMobil on the front lines of the increasingly dysfunctional arena surrounding energy, natural resource, and environmental policy across the country. Yet at the same time, we were hearing that other places around the world, like Colombia, were making huge changes, with previously inconceivable positive things happening as hundreds of millions—potentially billions—of people moved out of poverty and toward dramatically improved qualities of life, with better healthcare and living standards, improved environmental stewardship, and increased funding and technical capabilities for regulatory agencies. In Colombia alone, extreme poverty declined by half between 2002 and 2014. In 2016, more Colombians were considered to be middle class than in poverty,[1] and the gross domestic product grew 4.11 percent between 2001 and 2016.[2] Since the early 1950s, life expectancy at birth—now at 69 years—has risen by almost two decades.[3] As countries like Colombia make these strides, they experience improved health, education, and working conditions and can afford to take better care of their environment in the process.

ExxonMobil's interest in all of this was economic. Their economist had taken detailed growth and quality-of-life projections and modeled them into projections for future demand for bicycles, motorbikes, and personal automobile use in each region of the globe. This approach is core to the company's long-term planning, which is based on compilations of multiple data sources. This is one of the reasons that, over the past 100 years, ExxonMobil in its various corporate iterations (dating back to John Rockefeller's Standard Oil Trust) has consistently been among the world's most successful companies.

As the NCSL participants listened to Bill Gates's fireside chat presentation to state legislators gathered from around the country, like ExxonMobil, he painted a picture based on optimistic, glass-half-full thinking. Gates focused on needed changes to the US educational system, something under the direct purview of the gathered elected officials from around the country that day, and he was optimistic. Despite giving a talk citing many of the problems and inadequacies in the current US system, Gates focused on positive ideas for change. He communicated a message of hope for our educational system to those who largely set its standards and framework and appropriated the money to pay for it. His positive message contained ideas on how our system could provide even better modern educational opportunities for Americans of all economic and social backgrounds, including producing more critical thinkers who would grow up to be questioners and problem solvers rather than herd followers.

Returning to my room at the Grand Hyatt that evening, I followed my usual routine of turning on the television news while I caught up on hours of accumulated email. Scanning past the local public television channel, my attention was caught by a soft-spoken man named Wayne Dyer talking about something called *the power of intention*, describing how to think and live from a place of abundance rather than scarcity. After watching him go on for over an hour, I went online and ordered a program of his lectures, curious about his insights on the role of optimism in individual living, wondering what would happen if that approach were applied to societal decision-making, particularly in our political world, and to our most vexing environmental and natural resource issues.

Half full or half empty?

So much of today's news media coverage of world events and environmental and energy issues focuses on negativity. We see and hear stories about increasing global poverty and disparities in income, rather than progress being made as huge populations in countries like Mexico experience the benefits of significant economic growth. We hear about civil strife and protests in places like Brazil ahead of the soccer World Cup, rather than the rapidly improving Brazilian economy and entrepreneurial environment that have leapfrogged it into a rising star in biotechnology, addressing some of the world's most challenging health issues. The traditional media largely ignores the increasing stability, opportunity, and environmental stewardship in places like Brazil, Chile, and Colombia. On the political front, MSNBC runs "exposés" on big businesses and Republican politicians, Fox News' talking heads relentlessly attack liberals, and *The New York Times* churns out "special reports."

Yet are things really as bad as the media, politicians, activist groups, and even authors like me would have us believe? As *The Next Hundred Million* author Joel Kotkin[4] said in a presentation, the greatest entrepreneurial minds from around the world still want to move to places like the United States, Canada, Australia, and New Zealand. If things were as bad as much of the media would have us believe, it could lead us to give up on science and fact-based solutions. Yet if we look at the past, we see how such pessimistic outlooks have been proven wrong again and again. In the "11th hour," humankind inevitably finds ways to make things better. But we can only do so when we have a glass-half-full mentality. Few of us in the energy lobby at that 2005 Seattle conference foresaw the energy and associated economic renaissance that was already building like a huge wave about to crest and spread across vast regions of the United States itself, including Rust Belt states like Pennsylvania and Ohio.

While this American energy renaissance provided hope on the energy and economic front, what about the environmental front? The significant challenges associated with climate change require our serious collective attention. But rather than oversimplified bumper-sticker solutions, we need real plans, policies, and adaptations based on facts and science that will drive meaningful improvements in the human footprint—not throw-the-baby-out-with-the-bathwater approaches based on sky-is-falling headlines that often make things worse rather than better for the planet.

Breaking news!

How many of us have noticed that Fox, CNN, and MSNBC regularly put bold-lettered *Breaking News Headlines* across the screen, followed by serious and urgent-sounding news anchors with deep voices saying, "This just in"? A common tactic, it's meant to grab our attention. We stop what we're doing and focus on the sensational-sounding anchor, who is often just telling us something routine or sharing the opinion of a single expert. Yet media outlets use the sensational tactic to draw in our attention, thus increasing their ratings and ability to charge higher advertising rates, pure and simple.

This has been particularly true on environmental issues. Climate change, global warming, global cooling, the impending melting of the polar ice cap, and the predicted extinction of the iconic polar bears. After years of news media coverage of expert reports predicting the impending extinction of the polar bear, and ensuing filings by activist groups to have polar bears added to the list of endangered species with associated restrictions on their habitat—which is essentially almost the entire US Arctic—a rather unsensational news story reported that the US Fish and Wildlife Service found that polar bears were actually thriving in the Arctic offshore in the Chukchi Sea (one of the areas most impacted by polar ice cap decline).

So what if we all took the headlines about expert studies and predictions of doom as just data points and chose to make societal decisions from a place of the glass being half full rather than half empty? It raises questions about political actions like the cooperative pact that President Obama and Canadian prime minister Justin Trudeau signed early in 2016, with much fanfare and associated photo opportunities, that would establish a political process for placing further restrictions on human activity in the US and Canadian Arctic. Many people, including Native Eskimo leaders who live in the Arctic, said "not so fast" and asked if this was a political solution rather than a scientific one.

Abundance versus scarcity

In looking deeper at these issues, more and more people are asking tough questions and looking at the data on wide-sweeping pronouncements like the "peak oil" theory that so dominated US and European energy policy, politics, and perceptions for decades, starting in the 1970s. Peak oil has become a classic case of what happens when the societal herd acts out of fear and worst-case, scarcity thinking. For decades, politicians, activist groups, news media, and corporate interests positioned themselves as saviors from the end of modern society that would come as the world's oil ran dry. For decades, the societal herd stampeded behind expensive rules, restrictions, schemes, and subsidies to move us away from oil, largely based on fears sparked by peak oil and related pronouncements. Billions of dollars have poured out of our pockets—especially those of low-income people—into expensive programs and subsidies for wind, solar, and related power schemes. Too often, little evaluation is performed on the total environmental impact of producing and transporting the metals, cement, and associated materials needed to make and transport these expensive alternatives.

Real-world experience of the past decade now shows that the "peak oil" fears have turned out to be wrong, at least in their timing—by more than 100 years. As the old fears have faded, a new peak oil theory is evolving, and real change is coming to bear. The peak *demand* theory says that society is about to make transformational changes in energy use and efficiency through human ingenuity and innovation, rather than expensive subsidies based on crisis, sky-is-falling thinking. President Obama labeled oil as a "bridge fuel" during his unprecedented visit to Alaska's Arctic in 2015, just ten years after many of us at that gathering of energy lobbyists in Seattle lamented the political paralysis overtaking the US political system. Human ingenuity had turned the US energy situation 180 degrees—in spite of our political system. This change happened not because *Drill, baby, drill* politicians were in charge—in fact, just the opposite. It happened largely under a Democratic president—yet not because a Democrat was sitting in the White House or because Republicans controlled Congress, but in spite of that too. It happened because smart, innovative, science-based, environmentally sound development kicked in and found ways to produce needed energy, even in the midst of all of the societal and political chaos and paralysis. In fact, it led to an epic shift in energy production that probably surprised the world's largest energy companies just as much as anyone.

When I last did consulting work for ExxonMobil in 2006, if any of their internal experts had walked in and told their retiring CEO, Lee Raymond, or his incoming successor, Rex Tillerson, that within ten years, the United States would double production and possibly reemerge as the world's largest energy producer, they would have been dismissed as out to lunch. The same is true within other major energy companies like Shell, BP, and Chevron. For decades, US and European attitudes, policies, and beliefs on energy had been based on scarcity mindsets, beliefs, and policies about the inevitable end of affordable oil and gas energy sources, ever-shrinking production, and the associated economic decline. But as a result of human ingenuity, creativity, and innovation, a very different reality emerged.

Things can improve, despite the catastrophizing and fearmongering

The reality is that the United States is now experiencing a new phenomenon, energy abundance, rather than "peak oil" scarcity. US domestic production is at an all-time high, and the US oil boom is transforming the marketplace.[5] There have even been proposals to export surplus US energy to places as far away as the former Soviet Baltic countries via LNG (liquefied natural gas) tankers, something these countries badly wanted in order to be less reliant on Vladimir Putin's Russian energy sources. This creative concept would increase jobs and economic activity in the United States and divert energy purchases away from Putin's regime, which has used its energy revenues to fund ethnic unrest in Ukraine and the annexation of Crimea.

Places like North and South Dakota, Montana, and Pennsylvania have emerged as major new energy producers, creating not only jobs and economic activity but also the wealth that supports greater funding for public health and education. That production in the United States comes under the world's strongest environmental standards, with high-paying jobs, increased economic activity, and more revenue to pay for schools and education coming to the national treasury and to state and local governments in vast regions of the United States, many of which were economic laggards not so long ago. Manufacturing has even been reshored to places like the Northeast Rust Belt and previously backwater towns in Louisiana. This optimistically driven human ingenuity is reaching the rest of the world as well. Take, for instance, the story of the Malagasy man from chapter one, who sold jewelry made by local artisans in his roadside shop and was focused on using this as part of a bigger-picture approach to lifting up his entire society.

Never underestimate human ingenuity

This approach could be the bridge to a brighter future for both newly developing economies and well-established ones, and the catalysts for that transition may surprise many. More than 25 years after the *Exxon Valdez* disaster, I met former NATO Europe Supreme Allied Commander Joe Ralston, who told the story of being called to the Pentagon earlier in his careers and briefed on the then-top-secret concept of a plane that was invisible to radar and being told he was to be part of leading the team that would take this breakthrough technology from fantasy to reality at the height of the Cold War. The retired officer said the reaction from those who were briefed was excitement, and they looked forward to spending the next several years working on the concept, only to be told by the Pentagon briefers, "Gentlemen, we don't have years; you have a matter of months to get these flying."

That top-secret program led to what was known as the first stealth fighter, the F-117, put into flight in 1981. A classic case of breakthrough technology, this was achieved through human ingenuity, creativity, innovation, and determination. And this is the tip of the iceberg of what is possible when human innovation and ingenuity are put to the test. Just think what could happen if more of the same energy and creativity were used to bring people on different sides of environmental issues together to collaborate on more breakthrough innovations.

What if we just stop?

The genre of important scientific and technical solution finding is based on using science to understand and solve problems, not sky-is-falling advocacy. Scientific innovation is about finding technical and social breakthroughs to make things better. Activists saying "Stop this; stop that" are too often like people saying pure abstinence is the answer to stop the spread of HIV rather than investing in efforts to find a cure. What if all those working on all sides of mining and oil and gas development were focused on technological changes and breakthroughs and collaboration, rather than individual agendas?

We have a global opportunity to focus on making the economic pie bigger and on making the footprint of the pie tin, the apples, the dough, the oven, and even the energy it takes to heat the oven the most truly sustainable and environmentally responsible they can be.

4

How the Big Guy Can
Help the Little Guys Make
an Even Bigger Difference

As the leader of one of the most successful Native entities in North America met with Alaska's governor, they discussed the importance of balancing environmental protection necessary to preserve valuable subsistence fishing and hunting resources for his people with responsible economic development projects. These projects could provide critically needed funding for education and public health in the remote Northwest Arctic region of Alaska. Both had spent time with President Obama during his visit to the Native leader's Arctic region just weeks before and reflected on how so many other Native leaders had given the president the same message during his visit.

Growing numbers of Natives in the Arctic are speaking out about the need to keep capable and motivated young people in their villages and communities rather than standing by and watching the migration to urban areas with greater economic opportunity, better schools, and better healthcare. Without opportunity at the local level, this trend threatens local cultures and communities not only in parts of Alaska but also in places as far away as China, Central America, and Africa.

Balancing environmental stewardship and natural resource development was a theme that President Obama also shared in public messaging during his visit to Alaska's Arctic, a much-needed glass-half-full message. From my personal experiences over the past 30 years, the best way to help those who need it most, from residents in frigid bush areas of the North to people living in villages in the Central American heat and humidity of Belize and Guatemala, is through wise economic stewardship and the associated economic, societal, and entrepreneurial opportunity. As far too many people are living in challenging conditions on Indian reservations and other Native communities right here in our own backyards, the question is not *whether* we should provide opportunities to change that but *how*.

My work for the Boys and Girls Clubs to secure funding for teen suicide prevention furthered my own understanding of how young people in challenging situations and rural communities with disastrously high rates of obesity, diabetes, alcohol and drug addiction, and chronic abuse and neglect need hope. They need hope for a brighter future; hope for quality educations for themselves and their families; hope for healthy families, healthy diets, and healthy lifestyles; and hope for future generations.

The NANA regional Native corporation (successor to the Northwest Alaska Native Association) is one of the groups leading this movement toward hope. It is a case study in providing opportunity for thousands of Native shareholders. NANA has provided this hope for decades through their participation in a wealth-generating economic engine in Alaska's Arctic, one that has become the model for doing it right. As part owner and partner in the Red Dog zinc and lead mine in the remote Northwest Arctic since the late 1980s, NANA has been on the leading edge of finding balance among economic opportunity, environmental protection, and preservation of indigenous culture. An entire generation of NANA shareholders has grown up working at the mine, with associated wages and healthcare benefits, breaking the cycle of living on government welfare payments. They have to show up for work, meeting the same high standards for work performance and drug testing that are required throughout the industry—an important but often unspoken benefit of the high-paying jobs and opportunities that come with local participation and ownership in an increasing number of energy and minerals projects across Alaska, northern Canada, and Greenland.

When I went with a group of urban legislators from the cities of Anchorage and Fairbanks to tour what could be the second potential major mine project in the vast Northwest Arctic Borough (150 miles away from the Red Dog mine), many of the urban legislators carried preconceived notions that they would be met by people asking for political handouts, grants, and subsidies. Yet the local mayor greeted them by saying he and his people had their "hands up rather than their hands out." He said they were eager to bring forward ideas and projects to contribute to the state's economy rather than wait for the state to send money their way. The leaders of this remote area are focused on growing the opportunities for their people through wise natural resource development, as they themselves have already been empowered through their own experience with the economic engine of the Red Dog mine. They want to pass that on to future generations.

Sharing the wealth, health, and prosperity

In addition to the direct jobs and significant revenues from the Red Dog mine, NANA pays out dividends from mine earnings, not only to their own shareholders but also to tens of thousands of shareholders in other Native corporations across Alaska through revenue-sharing provisions under federal law. The NANA region of Northwest Alaska has one of the most successful and modern educational environments and school systems among remote communities and regions across the globe, also made possible by revenue from the Red Dog mine project paid to the local government and school district. NANA shareholders are better able to participate in traditional subsistence hunting, fishing, and berry-picking activities that are such an integral part of their culture, because they have cash income to support themselves and pay for fuel for their boats and snowmobiles.

The invasion of outsiders and modern society into remote regions across the globe brought change to generations of indigenous people. While many of us may romanticize the images from the old black-and-white movie *Nanook of the North*, the harsh reality is that the invasion of the modern world has brought both modern opportunities and modern challenges to the Arctic. It has brought aluminum skiffs, snowmobiles, and petroleum- and metal-based fishing gear, and we have increasingly encouraged Native peoples to rely on these tools of the modern world. With that reliance comes the need to pay for fuel to run boat and snowmobile engines in remote regions, where it is not uncommon to pay $8 or more per gallon for fuel. All of this is much more affordable when jobs and dividends come from Native corporations like NANA, and paychecks come from mines like Red Dog and modern oil and gas operations in the neighboring North Slope region.

Author photo: Utqiagvik, Alaska

In the case of Red Dog, not only does the mine provide economic opportunity for people of the region, but it also produces zinc. While maybe not a household word for many of us, zinc is commonly known for its use in alloys such as brass, nickel, and aluminum. Yet zinc has other qualities, most notably its use in many of the multivitamin supplements that we in the developed world take every day. It also has enormous potential to save lives in third- and fourth-world countries.

In fact, Teck Resources (the global mining company who operates the Red Dog mine in partnership with the NANA regional Native corporation) and the United Nations Children's Fund (UNICEF) Canada have entered into a partnership to save the lives of vulnerable children in India and elsewhere. The five-year program under the Zinc Alliance for Child Health (ZACH) targeted improving access to zinc supplements and oral rehydration salts to treat diarrhea while strengthening healthcare systems and improving supply chains across India. In announcing the partnership, UNICEF said that more children under the age of five die in India than anywhere else in the world. One of the leading causes of these deaths is diarrhea, and zinc supplements, combined with oral rehydration salts, are a proven and cost-effective treatment of diarrhea—yet less than 2 percent of Indian children have access to these life-saving therapies. UNICEF estimated that the program with Teck would save 100,000 children's lives in India over just a five-year period.

This initiative followed a 2009 UNICEF partnership with the Clinton Foundation, Teck, and other mining companies to combat diarrhea in Nepal and Peru. In announcing that initiative, former president Bill Clinton called for greater awareness and understanding of the importance of zinc in nutrition: "This is something 90 percent of us are unaware of or wouldn't have a clue as to what to do about it," he said.[1]

Red Dog mine operator Teck also joined the United Nations' Diarrhea and Pneumonia Working Group (DPWG), a global technical reference team for the UN Commission on Life-Saving Commodities for Women and Children. The DPWG is the only global coordinating body focused on accelerating access to treatment for childhood diarrhea and pneumonia, including zinc and oral rehydration salts. DPWG members include the Bill and Melinda Gates Foundation, the Clinton Health Access Initiative, the World Health Organization, and Teck partners UNICEF and the Micronutrient Initiative. Teck and the DPWG are now expanding the program for zinc and oral rehydration salts and are addressing bottlenecks in Ethiopia, Kenya, and India, three countries where Teck is supporting zinc scale-up projects through the Zinc Alliance for Child Health.[2]

From an environmental standpoint, despite predictions of environmental destruction when it was originally proposed decades ago, the Red Dog mine has actually cleaned up the creek that runs out of the mine area. For millennia, Red Dog Creek had runoff from the naturally occurring minerals in the area that made it toxic for fish—the same surface metals that originally attracted mining prospectors to the area. After decades of exploration, the mine and its associated modern, state-of-the-art water treatment facilities were developed through modern science and rooted in human ingenuity, and the water in Red Dog Creek is cleaner than ever. Fish thrive for the first time in centuries in the once naturally toxic creek.

Separating the "good guys" from the "bad guys"

Unfortunately, all too often, the media and special interest groups have created the impression that mines like Red Dog are always Armageddon for the little guy, especially indigenous peoples. Yet reality is increasingly the exact opposite. In the case of the Red Dog mine, years after it began operating, political operatives in Washington, DC, created something called the *Toxic Release Inventory Program*. While the term conjures up images of old factories with smokestacks billowing out plumes of black smoke and discharging toxic sludge into rivers and streams, in practice the TRI, when applied to projects like Red Dog, has become more about PR headlines than environmental protection, and the ensuing predictable media coverage has cited Red Dog as "ranked with the largest amount of toxic releases in the country for the past few years in a row."[3] A complicated system, the TRI counts any rock containing even minute amounts of naturally occurring toxins moved at a mine from the underground shaft or aboveground pit to another location at the site as a "toxic release" and thus a part of the "inventory"—even when the material isn't "released" into the air or nearby watersheds and even when it is placed in heavily regulated areas reclaimed to modern standards, using state-of-the-art science. Wildlife often thrives on top of the reclaimed, recontoured areas, which have been reseeded to grow native plants, such as this recontoured copper mine tailings hill in Miami, Arizona, with cattle grazing on the side of one of its hills.

Author photo

Done right, natural resource development offers unlimited opportunity to lift up the little guy and parts of society hit by the most challenging social and economic woes. A starting point in this approach is our thinking and adoption of a glass-half-full mindset to embrace both responsible natural resource development and environmental responsibility.

The spread of the glass-half-full approach

Using Red Dog and similar state-of-the-art projects as examples, we can look deeper into the question of poverty among Native Americans and indigenous people around the globe and billions of other people and apply critical thinking to find realistic approaches to turn that around. Some might lead people to think that more money alone can address these deep tragedies. If so, thoughtful people might ask where that money will come from in an era of government deficits not necessarily caused by any one political party or the other but by the increasing demands and wishes of an evolved society that wants to take care of everyone. With these demands come pressures on budgets for programs to benefit children, the disabled, the poor, and the disadvantaged. The question is how to address some of the worst poverty conditions on the planet while protecting the environment. Just maybe there is a way to make it rather than take it.

Following in the footsteps of Alaska Native groups participating in mining projects like Red Dog and energy projects on Alaska's Arctic North Slope, in January of 2013, the Crow Nation in Montana and Cloud Peak Energy Inc. signed an agreement for the potential development of the Crow tribe's coal resources—coal resources that could generate power to meet growing global demand and lift up a local struggling economy. At the time, Crow tribal leaders said a mine could provide a new source of revenue as the tribe deals with poverty and double-digit unemployment.

This approach followed by NANA and the Crow tribe to explore environmentally responsible natural resource development for the benefit of their people reminded me of something I encountered working on another potential mine project 500 miles away. One day in 2014, I participated in a community stakeholder visit to the potential project site along with an Alaska Native homemaker and grassroots thought leader from a fishing village. She had come to the site to learn more about the mine and about whether it could provide needed jobs for the region and balance that with strong environmental stewardship to protect the water quality precious to salmon in the regional watersheds.

For generations, her family had combined subsistence living with modern cash from a commercial salmon fishery during the short summer. Because that fishery was seasonal, income for the small community was limited to a few weeks each summer; year-round jobs were nonexistent. One of the biggest problems facing her Native community was young men walking around the village all day with their hands in their pockets, staring at their shoes, because they had nothing to do. This aimlessness largely stems from a chronic lack of opportunity, jobs, and associated self-esteem. All pieces of the equation lead to teen suicide epidemics in parts of rural Alaska with almost no functioning economies. It's a combination that the former head of the Alaska State Troopers once told me was often lethal and one of the biggest law enforcement challenges his officers face. If something could be done to provide year-round jobs, hope, and opportunity, the tide could be turned.

Self-determination

A growing number of Native corporations in Alaska, Indian tribes in other states, and First Nations groups in Canada are leading the way toward change and finding ways to transition out of a system of handouts from afar. Funding from faraway central governments in Washington, DC; Ottawa, Canada; and the European Union have become a way of life for many economically challenged rural regions across the globe. This has been the case for generations, from bush Alaska and Canada to South America, Asia, and Africa. When visiting Madagascar, a country where 92 percent of the population lives on less than $2 per day,[4] I was struck by the fact that the largest single building I saw in the entire country was the US embassy, an institution that stewards the flow of funding that props up much of Madagascar's struggling economy from halfway across the world in Washington, DC. This is well-intentioned economic assistance, but it is part of a system that keeps the country and its people stuck in a cycle of economic dependence. As Madagascar has struggled with the transition from French colonialism to communism, dictatorship to fledgling democracy, and then back to instability, patrons from afar have courted the huge island country with subsidies and handouts; Washington is just the latest.

Now, progressive local people in Madagascar are pursuing a very different approach to help the little guy, from the bottom up. People like the entrepreneur I described meeting in the last chapter, who was connecting local artisans with foreign customers, see the economic potential of environmentally responsible natural resource development as key to turning around one of the most impoverished countries in the world.

Greenland is also looking to move beyond that cycle of dependence, in which it relied on transfer payments and subsidies largely from its former colonial patron, Denmark, to prop up its people and economy and to pay for fledgling education and healthcare systems—until something changed. Learning from the experience of Native leaders in Alaska and Canada in determining their own economic and social destiny, more and more of Greenland's indigenous leaders have worked toward economic self-sufficiency and the associated true independence that comes with that. They are looking to their own mineral and energy resource wealth as the key to unlock that door and are taking matters into their own hands. As Laurence Smith described in a 2011 BBC *HARDtalk* interview about his book *The New North*, Greenland's leaders have increasingly told meddlers from faraway places like Europe, including environmental activist groups like Greenpeace and even oil companies like Shell, "Thanks for the input, but we're smart enough to figure this out for ourselves."

Taking multiple sources of data, just like ExxonMobil and other successful players in the energy and mineral resource world do, Greenland's leaders felt they were capable of taking charge of their own destiny rather than accepting the status quo. They could learn from the experiences of others how to balance natural resource development and responsible environmental stewardship while maintaining their subsistence hunting and fishing cultural heritage, which goes back thousands of years. With the economic means to afford this lifestyle in the modern world, they could set a new course for their people's future in the process.

Greenland's leaders chose to look into the future from a what-is-possible perspective. Along the way, they want to develop the economic means to fund modern schools like those in the Northwest Arctic region, provide modern healthcare, and balance economic opportunity with preservation of their traditional way of life. With this approach, they are striving to build hope for the future rather than continuing the spiral of depression and stagnation that too often comes with being a welfare society.

Greenland is following in the footsteps of its neighbors in Iceland and the Russian Far East region of Sakhalin Island by moving toward determining its own destiny and is further paving the way for places like Madagascar and Belize in the process.

Economic opportunity is a key to cultural opportunity

Culture is often an early casualty in a dying economy. In rural areas across the globe, local cultures, languages, history, and traditions often dwindle when younger generations migrate away and move to growing urban areas in search of greater opportunity. The incredible growth of the Chinese economy over the past two decades has been a case study in this dynamic. A well-known Chinese author and scholar told *The New York Times*, "Chinese culture has traditionally been rural. . . . Once the villages are gone, the culture is gone."[5] The massive Chinese migration to a growing number of supercities is taking people to where the jobs and economic opportunities are, and in the process, they often leave behind traditional cultures and customs.

Contrast that with my home state of Alaska, where regions with strong economies also have incredibly vibrant art and cultural communities, and those with stagnant or nonexistent economies have just the opposite. Where there are strong regional economies, local cultural festivals, theater companies, museums, and programs to preserve Native languages and history, Natives thrive, often with strong support from Alaska Native corporations, who derive much of their growing wealth from natural resource development under environmental regulation historically stricter than those in places like China. This is happening in regional hubs and small communities across the state. By thinking locally and acting globally, this glass-half-full approach can lift up entire societies, helping the little guy who needs it the most, and can benefit everyone from malnourished children dying from diarrhea in India to underemployed young Alaska Natives in the Arctic. Done right, this rising tide can lift all boats, including the planet's environment.

Author photos

5

Raising Up Entire Societies

Autism Speaks is the nation's leading advocate for families and individuals affected by autism and is a group that I have been proud to work for since 2012. Autism Speaks successfully advocated across the country for health insurance coverage of the most current applied behavioral analysis (ABA) therapies for treatment of autism spectrum disorders. Families now have access to the latest treatments and the associated opportunity for those impacted by autism to experience incredible progress. The combination of early intervention and the latest therapy leads to decreased need and costs for expensive longer-term (even lifelong) healthcare services. Autism treatment therapies resulted from human innovation, ever-advancing modern science, glass-half-full thinking, and funding to put them into practice. In Alaska, the economic means for that private and public sector funding comes from responsible natural resource development.

What if those who developed these breakthrough therapies had just thrown their hands up in defeat because there was too much opposition from interests entrenched in doing things the old way?

They might have given up because they encountered too many regulatory hoops to jump through, too many cultural biases to hurdle over, or too little funding to pay for the effort. Similarly, what if those looking to mine the materials that are used to make our smartphones, iDevices, hybrid cars, and modern medical equipment had thrown up their hands at some point and said, "Let's just stick with hundred-year-old techniques and technologies for mining these materials"? Everything is connected, and in making the world a better place for mankind through the provision of modern healthcare and technology, a core challenge is how to steward and develop our natural resources most responsibly and wisely to produce the components that make all of this work.

Four years after passage of an important bill to expand health insurance coverage for autism spectrum disorders, I took a large group of individuals affected by developmental disabilities, family members, and caregivers to meet with Alaska's governor to discuss disability-related issues. One of those who spoke up in the meeting was a man in his mid-20s who was studying political science at the University of Alaska. He shared the story of his lifelong struggle with autism and the impact it had on both him and his family as he was growing up. He had been subject to uncontrollable temper tantrums, unable to speak until he was a teenager. What if we had thrown our hands up on development of Alaska's natural resource wealth before he was provided with the latest autism treatments that were core to his transformation into a high-achieving college student speaking to the governor in a packed conference room? If he hadn't shared the story of his personal struggle, none of us would have had a clue that he had any sort of disability, much less one that delayed his ability to speak by a decade.

And what if he had been born in Madagascar?

Nineteen brothers and sisters, one dad, and three moms

The largely self-educated guide we had for several days on our 2013 trip through the northern jungles of Madagascar was in his mid-20s. He had been determined to find his way to what little employment opportunities were available in that economy, where 92 percent of the population makes less than $2 per day and where many children can never dream of ever attending school. At the end of our trip, we arrived in his hometown—the northern Madagascar port city of Antsiranana. As we exchanged farewells, we asked what his plans were after he dropped us at our gated hotel with armed guards posted in front.

He said he was going to a family meeting with his brothers and sisters, who met monthly to pass the basket to support their aging parents, "our dad and moms."

As the American teenagers in our group did a double take, he said, "That's right, my father was a polygamist, which was common in his generation." He then said, "It's actually a funny story. You see, my father followed Malagasy tradition after meeting my mother and went to her family home to meet with her father. When he arrived, a familiar young lady answered the door, and he asked her father for her hand in marriage."

After he was granted permission, another young girl walked into the room, and he realized he had asked for the wrong girl's hand in marriage. He continued, "That's where the story gets really funny. You see, my mother was one of three identical triplets, so my father, being a man of honor, asked to marry all three of them!"

Having as large a family as possible was important in his parents' generation, because in a financially poor country like Madagascar, there is no viable social security system, so the more kids people had, the better their chances of having offspring who would survive into adulthood and be able to care for them in their old age.

Yet what if one or more of those 19 brothers and sisters had been afflicted with autism or another severe health challenge? In a fourth-world country with an economy out of the Middle Ages that is still largely based on subsistence agriculture, the majority of the population even today has no electricity, heat, or running water, and most people cook and heat their homes with charcoal harvested from the heavily depleted local forests—a place where people still barter chickens for bananas and bread to survive. How could these people ever expect to get even the most basic care for a complicated condition like autism in a country like that? Certainly not through handouts from afar; as the US government and the EU are already propping up much of Madagascar's economy through aid payments and related programs, all of the handouts in Madagascar are already spoken for.

From laggards to leaders— the opportunities are limitless

Yet what if the organizer of the *"Madagascar et ses mines"* café I met on this trip and will talk more about later in this book was right, that modern mining could be the cornerstone building block for the future, serving as the basis for transforming Madagascar's economy, following the example of Chile? With a stronger economic base, growing countries can better afford modern healthcare and associated technology, and fourth-world laggards like Madagascar can leapfrog themselves into second- or first-world status just like Chile did.

A growing South American powerhouse with a natural resource endowment like Madagascar, Chile's average wage is now over $100 per day—50 times higher than in Madagascar.[1] Chile has leveraged mining as the engine driving its economy to diversify into other economic sectors like modern agriculture—including high-value products from some of the world's premier wine producers. Along the way,

Chile's leaders are striving to create an environment where students take responsible environmental stewardship to the next level, including the launch of a countrywide school-based environmental leadership initiative in 2011.[2]

If a potentially rising country like Madagascar could grow its economy and intellectual capabilities like Chile has done in just one generation, it can take advantage of modern technology and environmental practices in the responsible development of its natural resources, learning from the rest of the world. In doing so, Madagascar could transform its position from laggard to leader, using modern science and technology in resource and economic development. The resultant wealth could also allow modern healthcare and hope for people impacted by challenges like autism. In today's world, an optimistic and energetic country like Madagascar can take the healthcare knowledge of other places with large populations living in rural areas, apply them locally, tap the latest in human ingenuity, and combine leading-edge healthcare breakthroughs with modern technology from around the globe. In the case of healthcare issues like autism, countries like Madagascar can access the latest proven tools like the ABA therapies and make those available to their residents.

And they can do so without the expensive overhead costs that go with the legacy of the expensive US healthcare system. Countries like Mexico and Thailand are already doing this in other healthcare fields to the benefit of their residents—and even attracting a growing number of Americans seeking alternatives to expensive medical procedures and treatments in their home country, part of the growing trend toward "medical tourism." Through the use of modern technology, including the advent of telemedicine, the benefits of human ingenuity and breakthroughs in fields like autism treatment and other leading-edge healthcare services can be provided effectively and inexpensively in places like Madagascar.

Seem far-fetched? It's actually already being done at an accelerating rate around the globe, especially in places with large rural and indigenous populations like Alaska. Leaders there are seeing firsthand the benefits of applying a glass-half-full approach. For behavioral challenges like autism, parents and caregivers in Alaska are pushing for even more use of smartphone telehealth consultations for check-ins as an alternative to the expensive traditional approach of sending specialists out to patients' homes.

"I am astonished!" Those were the words of the chair of an Alaska Senate committee in response to testimony from the CEO of the Alaska Mental Health Trust Authority. The committee was considering a bill to allow individuals with disabilities, including autism, to establish individual savings accounts for disability-related expenses. Yet getting the Alaska program up and going so that people could help themselves by setting aside money in the equivalent of a health savings account or a college savings plan under the Federal Achieving a Better Life Experience (ABLE) Act required enabling legislation at the state level. In Alaska, that came with an estimated $100,000 startup cost for the state over the first two years at a time when Alaska, like so many other states, was grappling with huge budget deficits.

So, in stepped the CEO of the Alaska Mental Health Trust Authority, who felt the establishment of this program was so important that its board was willing to cover the cost of launching the program. It was able to do so because of the bigger pie created by natural resource development and the increased economic opportunities for the trust authority and its beneficiaries.

The framers of Alaska's state constitution over 50 years ago saw fit to specifically establish a mechanism for dedicating certain state lands with economic potential to a trust for mental health programs and their beneficiaries. Over time, as these lands have been responsibly developed for their resource potential, revenue generated by that activity benefits

Alaskans with developmental and other disabilities and mental health needs. The Trust now receives more than $5 million per year in revenue from the development of mineral resources. When combined with investment earnings on what has become a nearly $600 million trust fund, the revenues from this ever-growing pie support programs that benefit a staggering number of Alaskans—22,000 people impacted by mental illness, 13,000 people with developmental disabilities, 20,000 people with chronic alcoholism and other substance-related disorders, 5,000 people impacted by Alzheimer's disease and related dementia, and 12,000 people with traumatic brain injuries.[3] All of this was possible because money from environmentally responsible natural resource development was sustainably set aside, with a glass-half-full philosophy. This is how the Trust was in a position to shock the committee chair that day with the commitment of $100,000 to help launch the individual disability savings account program. Revenue from metal mining, coal mining, and oil and gas production is specifically directed toward helping people with challenges like autism as well as other physical, mental, and behavioral challenges.

Alaska is not the only place where leading-edge healthcare and healthcare technological breakthroughs are possible with the wealth produced through responsible development of natural resources. Alberta has one of the world's premier healthcare systems, also funded by the wealth created by the Canadian province's energy resources. Alaska's and Alberta's experiences are also shared with Norway, a country where the latest in technology, education, and healthcare is available to all of its citizens. A 2011 headline summed it up best: "Major oil finds shield Norway from economic gloom."[4]

Unfortunately, we too often see societal groupthink approaches that lead many toward believing glass-half-empty, worst-case theories like the "natural resource curse." The "curse" hypothesizes that natural resource development destroys third- and fourth-world countries, as well as economically depressed but resource-rich countries like Russia. While the data and case studies often cited as supporting evidence for the curse often conjure up worst-case scenario images of impoverished people in the third world and environmental Armageddon at industrial sites like the Norilsk Nickel smelters in Russia, my own experience in Russia uncovered a significant shift in that path.

For several years, beginning in the mid-1990s, I led a group of consultants in a region of Russia experiencing an economic boom as tens of billions of dollars flowed into energy projects developed by ExxonMobil and Shell on the Russian Far East island of Sakhalin. Our firm was involved in work ranging from advising some of the world's premier companies from Asia, Europe, and the United States looking to partner with Russian companies to getting work permits for Western oil company expat personnel from the KGB's successor (now known as the FSB), and I even did some work for a Clinton/Gore administration United States Agency for International Development (USAID) program training small Russian businesses and associations on how to lobby their own government. Those several years of consulting work took me around the world, including to ExxonMobil's home offices in Texas and Royal Dutch Shell's headquarters in The Hague and to countless meetings in their respective offices in Russia. Along the way, I participated in lengthy conversations with ExxonMobil and Shell in their early joint consideration of a new model for healthcare systems in remote places—using Sakhalin Island as a case study for what could be done differently.

Historically, in remote and third- and fourth-world places, major oil and gas and mining companies have followed a behind-the-walls approach to health and medical care, especially for their expatriate employees. Medical care for their expatriate employees was provided by doctors and nurses in clinics behind the walls of their company compounds, walled off from local residents. But in the mid- and late-1990s, several major oil companies joined together in developing guidelines for taking their health and medical care services outside the fences of their compounds to benefit local healthcare systems.[5] Their idea was that the money the oil companies spent on healthcare for their employees and families in these remote regions could be leveraged and spent in the local system. Doctors and specialists from around the world who provide healthcare for oil company personnel in remote regions would then partner with and mentor local providers, sharing modern practices and technologies—and would also share the revenue from healthcare contracts with the major oil companies.

In doing so, even more of the larger pie created by responsible natural resource development could be shared sustainably with local communities, regions, and even entire countries. Shell's operating company took the next step and implemented this model on Sakhalin Island, contracting with the diagnostic clinic in the capital city of Yuzhno-Sakhalinsk to provide care for Shell's Russian employees, giving the diagnostic center the opportunity for new revenue from an anchor contract with Shell to expand services for other local residents in the remote city of 170,000 people.

I visited Yuzhno-Sakhalinsk multiple times over that five-year period, where schoolteachers and other public employees were previously paid little more than subsistence wages, if they were paid at all. Just imagine living in a place where poorly paid doctors and schoolteachers never knew whether they were even going to get a paycheck. Then with the economic infusion of ExxonMobil and Shell's investments of billions of dollars in Sakhalin's energy projects, the region experienced rapid economic growth, more revenue to support public services, and hope for a better future. Along the way, this shift also produced the means to start cleaning up the environmental messes left behind by decades of unchecked oil production during Russia's communist era, as well as more resources for education and public health and parks and recreation facilities.

Progressive political leaders like President Obama, following in Al Gore's footsteps in bringing Western oil development to Russia's Sakhalin Island, have advocated for the use of this model to help other struggling economies in some surprising places around the globe to get on their feet.

Seventy percent of an entire country mapped for its mineral resource potential

"Mineral wealth could uplift an entire country," stated a press release from top Obama administration officials,[6] and with great fanfare, an impressive US government multiagency, multiyear effort culminated in the announcement that modern, state-of-the-art technology led by the US Geological Survey had mapped 70 percent of an entire country's mineral potential. The result was cited by US officials in 2012 as a "treasure map" of potential mining projects, particularly large-scale copper and gold prospects.

The US government analysis indicated that the tax revenues to this particular country could be in the billions of dollars each year, an amount representing exponential increases in its federal budget. Direct employment from mining development was estimated by US officials to be potentially half a million people, an astonishing number in a place where the average annual income is just $1 per day—half of that of even Madagascar. These mining jobs and the associated service and support positions would be the highest paying in the private economy of the country. With the head of the national mining department citing the associated infrastructure development (road systems, rail lines, electricity transmission lines), one can only imagine how many secondary and support jobs would be created by this large-scale mineral development. It has the potential to completely transform the entire economy and create opportunity to uplift millions of people out of poverty in the country of . . . Afghanistan!

Yes, that's right, a multiagency team of US government agencies, led by the Department of Defense and the US Geological Survey, completed an unprecedented geological evaluation of Afghanistan. Obama administration agencies led the evaluation, and subsequent promotion, of not only the copper and gold potential of the country but also its oil and gas potential. Senior Obama administration officials saw that helping lift Afghanistan out of poverty was in the US national interest: A stronger economy would help lift the entire country out of its decades-long death spiral. The social good, poverty alleviation, stronger economy, and thus more functional society and government was believed to be critical to the interests of US and European allies in preventing Afghanistan from again deteriorating into a breeding ground for terrorist activities. The US government determined that full-fledged, aggressive development of mineral and oil and gas resources was the best way to lift up the entire nation's struggling economy and that it could be done in an environmentally responsible way. This is the same approach that President Obama took to Brazil in 2011, when he led a trade mission to promote offshore oil and gas development in Brazil's Atlantic Ocean.

The US government program to promote development of Afghanistan's mineral and oil and gas "treasure" was largely completed under the leadership of the Obama administration, although it was originally started under the Bush administration. These two US presidents have been defined by the mass media as being so opposed on a vast array of policy issues, including defense, economic policy, and natural resource development—all central components of this Afghanistan initiative—but they were in lockstep alignment on the vast potential benefit of environmentally responsible development of Afghanistan's copper, gold, oil, and gas resources for the people of the country.

Responsible environmental policy has become a landmark of the United States in recent decades. The United States has been a global leader for decades in establishing many of the highest environmental standards on the globe, standards which have been used as a template in other countries.

Clearly, policy advisors to both President Bush and President Obama saw that science, public policy, and responsible mineral development can be done right and can lift up entire third- and fourth-world economies in the process. Afghanistan, like Madagascar, might follow in the footsteps of countries like Chile, using mining development as the basis for moving the entire country into the developed world in an incredibly short period of time—to the benefit of the citizens, healthcare, education, and quality of life.

What if our collective global thinking was based on recognizing and maximizing the potential of responsible stewardship of this wealth around the globe? What could happen to per capita income, funding for quality education, public health, and environmental protection? The potential is endless when viewed as a glass half full, especially when political leaders around the world stop catering to special interest agendas that are herding us away from the real finish line. Just think what could happen if we did this thoughtfully, with the best modern science and technology, in our own backyards.

6

Increasing Wealth Can
Increase Environmental Protection

I've been to some rough areas, including Egypt's Sinai Peninsula in the summer of 1984, when Muammar Khadafy's agents were mining the Suez Canal, blowing holes in huge oil tankers. Machine-gun-toting Egyptian soldiers stopped us at numerous checkpoints on the one-lane highway across the desert. UN peacekeepers were the only other people we saw snorkeling in the Red Sea. I was in central Dublin during The Troubles in adjacent Northern Ireland, when 20-plus-percent unemployment was accompanied by warnings from locals not to wander a block in the wrong direction—even in broad daylight. I was in Bucharest, Romania, during the communist era, where a soldier with a bayonet on the end of his machine gun stood guard at the smoky airport bar, overlooking the tarmac where German shepherds patrolled around the parked planes looking for stowaways. I attended countless meetings in Russia after President Yeltsin disbanded the government in 1999, and heavily armed guards were commonplace at hotels, shops, and banks. Yet none of these compare to Belize City during the summer of

2012. Once an environmentally rich and economically thriving British colony overlooking the Caribbean, it was now a dangerous and downtrodden nightmare with rampant crime and pollution.

The online travel advisories and numerous warnings from friends and colleagues who had been to the Central American port city didn't do justice to what I encountered during my volunteer work there developing a strategic fundraising plan for Belize's National Organization for the Prevention of Child Abuse and Neglect (NOPCAN). While staying in the relatively safe mountain town of San Ignacio, I was given warnings even from locals before I traveled into Belize City for meetings with NOPCAN's director at his office behind the security gates at the city's central hospital. During a broad-daylight van ride from San Ignacio into central Belize City, the driver pointed out a group of children, who could not have been older than 14, riding small bicycles through the downtown traffic.

He said, "Those are the ones to watch for, as they will rob someone and shoot them without giving it a second thought."

I was not sure whether to be reassured or on even higher alert when he said not to worry; he carried a gun larger than theirs under his driver's seat just in case. He then called someone he had been in a traffic accident with days before, who he said "had dangerous friends." He said that after he dropped me at my hotel, he was going to meet the guy and give him an agreed-to amount of cash rather than go through Belize's corrupt court system or, worse yet, be awoken in the middle of the night by the other driver's gun-toting friends.

The driver dropped me off at the Princess Hotel, which on Expedia looked to be a modern oceanfront resort gem overlooking the Caribbean. In reality, it symbolized so much of the country's downward spiral. While it did have waterfront beaches "overlooking the turquoise waters of the Caribbean," it felt like a façade, given that the huge hotel was virtually empty, and its abandoned swimming pool seemed more like a monument to past dashed hopes than a tourist destination, overlooking a trash- and litter-covered shoreline.

Author photos

The trash on Belize City's beach was worse than I had seen anywhere else in the world. I disregarded the security warnings, and an afternoon walk along the coastal Barrack Road outside the gates of the hotel revealed an oceanfront drive on par with many beachfront cities on the French or Spanish Rivera. The shoreline drive winds past apartment buildings overlooking the Caribbean, a beautifully designed coastal setting left behind from the British colony; it included an ideally situated beachfront park, where a pair of well-dressed police officers sat at a picnic table in the empty park, twiddling their thumbs in the afternoon sun.

Yet what seemed most odd was that this beautiful beachfront city park was abandoned on a sunny afternoon, especially in what had once been a relatively middle-class country. Belize's chronic un- and underemployment seemed to go hand in hand with all of the accumulated ocean trash piled up on the beach—plastic bottles and bags, old motor oil cans, and abandoned tires all lining the shoreline in the afternoon sun.

A former British colony that had once been an island of stability during the Central American civil and economic unrest of the 1970s and 1980s, Belize has since sunk into an economic, social, civil, and environmental abyss. As neighboring countries have experienced solid economic growth in recent years, those places can now afford the stronger environmental stewardship that comes with the economic means to maintain parks, clean up beaches, and pay park rangers. Yet Belize continues to sink under the weight of an economic concession system left behind by the British, with a few wealthy interests controlling many of the country's potential economic engines. Limited groups control dairy production, citrus growing, logging (both legal and illegal), and consumer goods. Most prominent is the concession to one company for virtually 100 percent of the country's beverage distribution system. You can be in the central Belize City port or on the back roads through the jungle, and the choices are limited to their own Bilikin Beer, Heineken, or the Coca-Cola they distribute exclusively countrywide—virtually no Pepsi products, local microbrews, or Coors to be found anywhere.

As the populations of Belize and other Central American countries have grown, the need to protect their ecosystems from overfishing, overlogging, and unregulated mining has become more important than ever. As these populations increase, so do the needs of local people for daily living, which places greater pressure on their natural resources and increases the need for a modern, environmentally and economically efficient economy to support them. But Belize has just the opposite problem, with a social and economic malaise that stifles innovation and entrepreneurship due to its closed-market concession system. This system destroys the hopes of young people for a better economic future, stifles innovation, and leads to a collective blaming of the country's ongoing troubles on a few rich power brokers and allegedly corrupt government officials. As a lifelong Belizean taxi driver told me, the country's problems were all due "to our government leaders, who thieved [sic] all the money."

With all of Belize's problems come social troubles, including the highest rates of HIV/AIDS in the Central America and Caribbean region and widespread apathy toward the environment—evidenced by the prevalent coastal and roadside trash throughout the country. This apathy also stifles the country's economy, creating an inability and unwillingness to afford stronger environmental stewardship, all while their neighbors are thriving.

Across the border

Belize is a country stuck in a collective "who cares" mentality, and it has the results to show for it. Going on a trip over the mountain roads into neighboring Guatemala by taxi and crowded public shuttle van, I had prepared for the worst, especially based on the harsh online descriptions of a chaotic border scene, where the bridge over the Mopan River divides the two countries. Yet upon crossing over the bridge into the Guatemalan border town of Melchor de Mencos, a vastly different feeling was pervasive. This was a country not so long ago mired in a 36-year-long civil war, but the Guatemala I found was bustling with energy. Unlike the Belizean side of the border, there was activity everywhere—people hustling to and from markets, banks open with modern ATMs on the corners of dirt streets, children kicking around soccer balls.

Once we packed into the public minivan for the drive to the Guatemalan national park at the ancient Mayan city and temples of Tikal, a UNESCO World Heritage Site, I noticed something else was very different from neighboring Belize. The two-lane national highway had been freshly paved, and as we drove farther into Guatemala, there were numerous large fields along the highway through the rainforest, virtually all filled with something that at first appeared to be sugar cane. A closer look revealed they were jungle grasses rapidly reclaiming the rainforest from small farms that had been abandoned. *The New York Times* described this trend in a 2009 story:

> In . . . tropical countries around the world, small holdings . . .— and much larger swaths of farmland—are reverting to nature, as people abandon their land and move to the cities in search of better livings.
>
> These new "secondary" forests are emerging in Latin America, Asia and other tropical regions at such a fast pace that the trend has set off a serious debate about whether saving primeval rain forest—an iconic environmental cause—may be less urgent than once thought. By one estimate, for every acre of rain forest cut down each year, more than 50 acres of new forest are growing

in the tropics on land that was once farmed, logged or ravaged by natural disaster.[1]

After driving for hours through those farms being reclaimed by the jungle and reaching the national park at Tikal, I was struck by how clean and highly organized the park was. There was no trash, unlike the parks in Belize, and at Tikal, there were park rangers who were busily engaging with visitors, not twiddling their thumbs. Most of all, there was a general feeling of optimism and activity. The World Bank reports, "Thanks to prudent macroeconomic management, Guatemala has been one of the strongest economic performers in Latin America in recent years, with a GDP growth rate of 3.0 percent since 2012, and nearly 4.0 percent in 2015."[2]

My time in the Guatemalan lakefront city of Las Flores, near Tikal, revealed a modern airport and a peninsula filled with small three-star hotels, waterfront restaurants, cathedrals, and European-feeling architecture. Las Flores was catering to Guatemalan and other Central American visitors rather than foreign tourists from the United States or Europe. This local tourism is part of a regional trend toward growth in places like Guatemala as their economies move away from slash-and-burn, high-impact subsistence farming and toward greater economic opportunities, benefitting the environment in the process, with 70 percent of its rainforests now in protected land management status.[3] Guatemala's improving economy has also led to an improvement in policing of more than just its parks; murder rates have declined steadily in recent years as the country's government institutions and services have become more solid, in stark contrast to neighboring Belize.[4]

Done right, resource development creates the wealth for modern environmental protection. In Belize, this hasn't happened yet because the country and its leaders have lacked vision and commitment for using their abundant natural resources to benefit their citizens while protecting their environment rich in jungle rainforests, coastal waterways inhabited by graceful manatees, and spectacular coral reefs. These environmental assets have all suffered under a lack of strong regulatory management, with associated overharvesting of forests and fisheries, and have been hit hard in a situation where no one reliable is in charge, exacerbating the country's free fall.

Strong environmental stewardship is made all the more important in today's world, with growing global population and the associated needs of people for metals and energy for daily living. Strong environmental stewardship is easier when there is more wealth to afford to do things right. And done right, increased wealth can lead to economically empowered rather than impoverished societies. Responsible development is the strongest route to providing a better quality of life, more parks, and better environmental protection and stewardship.

7

Living with a Collective Mentality of Abundance Rather Than Scarcity

Looking through a glass half full, rather than one half empty, can change everything—especially how we deal with environmental questions, challenges, and opportunities. Working toward the collective good is something I have seen succeed repeatedly in 30-plus years of involvement with natural resource and environmental political issues. Those who are playing not to lose too often let fear dominate their thinking. Negativity tends to bring everyone down.

As humans, we naturally migrate toward places and people who foster positive environments and away from those who are negative and unengaged. A good friend of mine used to be in senior management at Starbucks, and he once told me that their biggest competitor was not other large chains but individual local coffee shops, where the baristas have smiles on their faces, positive attitudes, and often remember customers and their usual orders by name. Cultivating that sort of positive attitude and can-do approach thrust Starbucks from one small shop at Pike Place Market in Seattle, where its founder wanted to recreate the European neighborhood café experience, into one of the world's largest and most successful companies.

Think about how we react when political leaders give messages of optimism and inclusion and have a can-do attitude. In contrast, consider how often we allow our own thinking to slip into negativity when politicians attack each other and anyone else with differing political views, like both Donald Trump and Hillary Clinton did in the 2016 presidential election campaign. Negative thinking leads to negative results for all of us. As the Dalai Lama says, "In order to carry a positive action, we must develop here a positive vision."

The power of positive thinking

When we turn negative thinking around, we can see limitless opportunities for good. A happier society fosters healthier families, healthier communities, and healthier institutions. In societies where people are encouraged to pursue their dreams, they are more creative. Creativity is the basis for innovation, and with that creativity comes more positive ways of living and glass-half-full mindsets based on abundance rather than scarcity. Those abundant mindsets inspire architects to design more creative buildings and inspire communities and cities to build more parks and green spaces, keep their communities cleaner, and drive an upward spiral. When this happens, typically drab transportation infrastructure is designed differently, like the expansion of Interstate 90, running east from downtown Seattle through Mercer Island. This freeway now includes overpasses with bright green trees, parks, and even sports fields on top of them.

In previous chapters, I shared many of my experiences traveling through Madagascar, Russia, and Belize. These countries are on opposite ends of the world, with different cultures, economies, languages, and spiritual beliefs—and each with a distinct and very different ethos.

Belize is a country whose collective ethos is marred by apathy—toward the environment, toward innovation, toward the country's leaders, and toward the future. Its collective apathy is a key reason why a country that once had one of the strongest economies, environmental stewardship systems, educational levels, and functioning democracies in the region has descended into an abyss. Blessed with a beautiful natural environment, Belize remains a model of diversity, with four different cultural groups with rich heritages living side by side. Yet despite all of this, Belize has few leading artists, writers, scientists, athletes, or entrepreneurs. The country's underlying apathy has made it most notable for its crime rates, which includes one of the highest murder rates in the world.

Russia is a country that was gripped for nearly a century by oppression and fear. Nearly a century of totalitarian rule led to a culture of pervasive glass-half-empty thinking. Most over-50-year-old Russians I worked with had pervasive glass-half-empty mindsets. They were products of a society that cut down anyone who was viewed as being too successful.

This mindset is summed up by a Russian folk story about two dairy farmers. One of the farmers was successful enough that he bought a second cow. When the neighboring farmer saw that, he shot one of his neighbor's two cows. Leaving the remaining cow alone, he declared, "There. Now we are all equal again!"

Russia's collective glass-half-empty mindset is an underlying reason why the world's largest country, which is filled with a natural resource wealth that includes some of the world's largest mineral and energy deposits, has been a chronic economic and environmental underachiever. With one of the world's most highly educated populations in natural sciences, mathematics, physics, chemistry, and engineering, unemployment and underemployment remain chronic. Entrepreneurship and creativity were stifled for generations, and a society with so much potential was left with a Soviet-era legacy of drab, rusted-out, trash-laden, heavily polluted industrial cities spanning its 11 time zones. The country still struggles with a legacy of reckless Soviet-era natural resource and heavy industry development.

When I started working in the Russian Far East in 1997, it was common for drivers to have PhDs. I met a man driving for Exxon's Russian affiliate who had his in art history. The Russians I met over the course of the ensuing five years were products of a society where virtually any positive-thinking, innovative entrepreneur had escaped the country whenever they could. This innovation and entrepreneurial brain drain of epic proportions left behind a country with disastrously high rates of alcoholism, obesity, heart disease, and death—and a low birth rate to top it off. The dramatically shrinking population was forecast to go from 149 million in 1995 down to less than 100 million in our lifetimes.[1]

Contrast glass-half-empty Russia and who-cares-about-the-glass Belize with glass-half-full Madagascar. Although the country is consistently ranked as one of the ten poorest countries, I found Malagasy people during my visit to be proudly proclaiming, "We might be the world's 173rd richest country, but we are the world's happiest." One of the reasons for that happiness is an underlying cultural optimism, despite Madagascar's ongoing economic and political instability. Much of the traffic is still human-powered: People pull rickshaws and heavy carts laden with supplies, often barefoot. And the majority of the population does not have electricity, heat, or running water or sewers. Yet Madagascar shows a remarkable lack of roadside and beachfront trash, in contrast with Russia and Belize.

At the bridge over the Mahavavy River in northern Madagascar, I saw a group of hustling young men repairing and refurbishing bicycles, creating something out of what many of us would consider virtually nothing and not wasting a single spare part. In a nearby region, when our van drove along a one-lane dirt road to get to the Ankara bush camp, we passed countless collections of huts cut off from the modern world and even several hours walk from the nearest paved road. As our SUV drove past, kicking up dust along the way, we passed group after group of young kids, who waved at us enthusiastically yelling, "Hello, vassar! Hello, vassar!" Our guide translated that to "Hello, boss! Hello, boss!" That was a term of respect, left over from the colonial period, when white Frenchmen were actually the bosses, and it remains a term many rural Malagasy still use to describe European visitors. Asking what we should do when the kids yelled that out and waved, he said, "Wave back, of course."

Throughout Madagascar, we met happy, friendly people, including several entrepreneurial young Malagasy, none of whom were determined to get out of the country like those in Russia during its economic decline or sitting around sharing tales of woe like so many I met in Belize. Instead, these young Malagasy were trying to change their country from within, from the bottom up. And they felt free to talk about the need for change, opportunity, improved healthcare and education, and the preservation and celebration of their traditional cultures openly, without fear of oppression or of upsetting societal norms. The bustling capital of Antananarivo, a city bursting at the seams, had grown from 700,000 people to a population approaching two million in just the two decades between 1993 and 2013. I read that it was on the US and EU travel advisory watch lists due to political unrest and rising threats of crime—just like Belize—yet I saw only a small number of police and soldiers during our travels. It felt very different from Belize.

We can all learn a lot from Madagascar's optimistic people and positive approach to life—a culture where positive-thinking entrepreneurs like the Malagasy café owner are working to make things better for the country. If Malagasy optimism, creativity, and determination can tap modern technology and know-how, that combination could lead to breakthroughs in bettering the planet and its people that could be a model throughout neighboring Africa and other parts of the world. Even in the United States, we can learn more about how to better meld the planet and the environment.

An optimistic mindset sets the stage for innovation, creativity, and responsible, sustainable economic development, particularly in minerals and energy. With that can come more funding for crucial education and public health programs—just as the Alaska Mental Health Trust Authority has done with revenue from natural resource development on its lands that have been dedicated to funding programs for mental health and disabilities for tens of thousands of Alaskans.

In a time when so many of us have been conditioned by glass-half-empty collective societal guilt about use of day-to-day products and modern conveniences in a consumer-gone-mad society, there is a better path. Wise use of natural resources is prudent, and responsible societies that do it wisely can create larger economic pies. Consumer trash can end up in tightly regulated and monitored landfills rather than on the sides of the road, and those landfills are often later converted into green spaces and parks. This is in stark contrast to the smoldering trash piles I saw in Russia's Yuzhno-Sakhalinsk, where cows grazed on refuse at the edges of the dump, and with Belize City's trash-littered shorelines.

Limiting or limitless environmentalism

At the end of the day, there are two ways to approach environmental and resources issues: with a limiting or limitless mindset. One sets the stage for limitless innovation, creativity, and prosperity for humans and the environment moving forward; the other limits us to us-versus-them thinking, antagonism, stagnation, deprivation, and ultimately environmental destruction and devastation.

8

Think Differently

The bus ride from Iceland's Keflavik International Airport into the capital city of Reykjavik takes just over an hour on what looks like a brand-new four-lane highway to the city center, downtown bus terminal, or over 160 modern hotels and guesthouses throughout the city. Icelandair and discount airline WOW Air operate some of the newest, most brightly painted, clean aircraft fleets around. They have made Iceland a new air crossroads of the world, connecting Europe and North America with a strategic and efficient system of flights. This is all part of Iceland's innovative model of taking advantage of its geographic position, natural resource wealth, and modern technology to integrate with the economies and cultures of the entire world— transforming Iceland from a remote, isolated, wind- and rain-swept island in the middle of nowhere to a global center.

Iceland's resurgence following the global economic crash in 2008 is nothing short of a miracle. This transformation was made possible through the country's collective ingenuity, can-do spirit, and positive thinking. Icelandair's own people symbolize this positive attitude, including flight attendants and pilots who offer a unique "stopover buddy" system. The airline encourages passengers to stay over for multiple days when they change planes at Keflavik on their way between North America and Europe, during which they can "buddy up" with Icelandair employees, who serve as local hosts for unique Icelandic experiences. Pilots will take visitors heli-skiing, flight attendants lead culinary expeditions through Reykjavik's stunning array of top-notch restaurants, and passengers can buddy up for mountain biking or a trip to a local yoga studio. Icelandair's website says to participate, "the only requirement is a decent amount of curiosity and courage."

All travelers to Iceland are encouraged to visit the world-famous Blue Lagoon hot springs, its most popular tourist attraction. Sitting in the middle of vast lava fields between the airport and the Reykjavik city center, the Blue Lagoon is considered unnatural, because it is the result of an industrial accident. Crews drilling for geothermal energy resources accidentally punctured a volcanic aquifer filled with silicon-laden hot water. Being a society of hearty, humorous, and creative people by nature, Icelandic entrepreneurs turned the accident into an artificial lagoon, forming a huge, steaming turquoise pond. Now a unique tourist destination, it feels like the United Nations of hot tubs, filled with laughing Japanese, Brazilian, European, American, and Canadian visitors.

Iceland's innovative tapping of its natural geothermal resources was also the catalyst for another unique sight out the window on the luxury bus ride through the lavascape between the airport and city center. We passed a building larger than a Boeing or Airbus airplane factory hanger with no smokestacks or other outward signs of activity besides a transport ship anchored just offshore connected to a conveyor.

When I asked a local what it was, he energetically responded, "One of the world's largest aluminum smelters!"

Having worked on many controversial mineral resource projects over the years, I was intrigued. It turns out that innovative Icelanders have taken advantage of their unique position adjacent to global shipping routes, combined with their abundant geothermal and hydropower energy resources, to attract three large metal smelters to their island nation—something Icelanders I met were proud of. Spread strategically in three different regions, they take ore from mines all over the world and, using the energy-intensive smelting process, refine raw ore into metals used by all of us in modern society. This is all done with the latest modern technology and one of the lowest carbon footprints of any facility of their kind on the planet—a stark contrast to the images of environmental Armageddon in places like the Norilsk Nickel Smelter complex in Russia and Baotou, China.

Iceland's metal smelters provide the economic engine and foundation for transforming the country's economy from one based on old-school high-seas fishing and limited agriculture to a modern global trading, technology, and financial center. Renewable energy sources power the huge smelters that drive an increasingly diverse economy filled with high-paying jobs. Using that energy abundance and geographic position adjacent to the Atlantic fiber-optic cables that connect North America and Europe, can-do Icelanders are expanding their economy deeper into high technology, including efforts to host cloud-computing technology in Iceland. The energy-intensive collections of server machines that are the backbone of the cloud generate extensive heat and also must be located near global fiber-optic connections like those subsea cables that run past Iceland. In further connecting these dots, Icelanders have turned their consistently cold environment into an asset. With these sorts of innovative projects based on a positive approach, Iceland now has almost zero unemployment and one of the highest per-capita university enrollment rates on the planet.

Iceland is a place where it is just as likely to be 45 degrees, rainy, and windy in June as in January. Yet the country is also fortunate to have a culture that spurs leaders who embody creative thinking and optimism beyond big industrial and technology business opportunities to the tourism and transportation sectors, as well as to social challenges facing youth across the world today. *The Atlantic* wrote that the percentage of Icelandic teens who had been drunk in the past month "plummeted from 42 percent in 1998 to 5 percent in 2016 . . . while the percentage who had ever used cannabis dropped from 17 percent to 7 percent, and those smoking cigarettes fell from 23 percent to 3 percent" so that "Iceland tops the European table for the cleanest living teens."[1]

Social scientists and others who have examined this trend credit much of it to a countrywide initiative to build sports and recreation facilities, chess programs, and arts and music facilities for youth in Iceland and to a cultural commitment of parents and adults engaging with school-age kids in the afternoons and evenings. This combination has been made more possible through Iceland's strong economy, which funds these facilities and programs, and through employment for parents who are increasingly engaged in higher-value work opportunities during the day.

Those same geothermal hot water resources that provide huge volumes of affordable power for the aluminum smelters and the steamy water for the Blue Lagoon also provide heat to Reykjavik residents in their modern homes. The natural geothermal hot water is carried in a vast system of underground water lines throughout the city and, along the way, is tapped for the city's network of public swimming pools and water parks that are core to those youth facilities and programs.

Central Reykjavik itself is a cultural hotbed, with an active international arts community and a vibrant theater and music scene. It has one of the world's most beautiful modern libraries, a unique and architecturally impressive waterfront civic center, and modern restaurants on par with those anywhere else in the world. Icelanders have also preserved Reykjavik's unique historical architecture, giving the city a feel something like a hybrid of Copenhagen, rural Scotland, and San Diego. Its streets are filled with modern and historical sculptures and statues, with designated bike lanes and paths throughout, reminiscent of Amsterdam, along with several world-class golf courses as scenic as any on the planet.

Iceland's political system is also unique. Following the collapse of its economy in 2008, political leaders were part of the country's economic renaissance that, in a few short years, put the country back on its feet, with Reykjavik even electing a professional comedian as mayor. Iceland is a place where the country's first-ever advancement to the heralded Round of 16 in the 2016 European soccer championships received more headlines and press coverage than their election of a new president.[2] This contrasts sharply with the increasingly polarizing, us-versus-them, Roman gladiator environment of US politics.

By changing our individual and collective thinking here in North America, we can do even more and take this approach even further than Iceland due to our larger population, more extensive natural and human resource base, greater educational resources, and larger entrepreneur base. If we do, we can find endless opportunities to increase emotional and physical wealth and opportunity and can continue to advance our collective care for the planet. If we think differently, we can increase environmental stewardship and improve our quality of life. If remote Iceland can build some of the world's largest aluminum smelters using hydro and geothermal power, have virtually zero unemployment, double university enrollment in a decade, and see rates of teen alcohol and drug abuse plummet, the rest of the world should pay careful attention.

When we think differently, we behave differently. As new environmental technologies and new resource development projects are proposed, we can gather around the table and work together on how to make them better, rather than sitting across from each other, finger-pointing and laying blame. There are more technological advances when people collaborate and brainstorm than when they attack each other. Following Iceland's example, a more positive approach can lead to incredible breakthroughs in doing things right across the globe. The opportunities are endless as we shift our thinking away from fear-based decision-making into hope and optimism.

9

Improving How We Think
and Teaching to Think

Gallup CEO Jim Clifton addressed a gathering with a positive message about the importance of mentoring and connecting people in today's world. He illustrated the serendipity of leaders who had simply connected those with big ideas with those who could turn those ideas from dream to reality, including the story of Al Gore's brief conversation with a Pentagon engineer who told Gore of his vision for the potential social and economic benefits of making the Advanced Research Projects Agency Network (ARPANET) available for public use. This chance meeting led then-Senator Gore to sponsor the Supercomputer Network Study Act of 1986 and the subsequent High Performance Computing Act of 1991, two laws that helped establish the framework for the Internet. This was a societal advance that led to one of the biggest transformations in human history.

Just as Gore played a vital role in the launch of the Internet, he played a role in those deals I discussed earlier in this book to develop massive oil and gas resources offshore in the Russian Far East. When government leaders like Gore connect idea makers with those who can launch the ideas, whether it is the global Internet or oil and gas projects in Russia, it is often done because the idea has merit for the societal good. Al Gore certainly didn't put his deal-making for Exxon and Shell into the public spotlight during the ensuing 20 years, indicating that his motivation for leading this pro-business initiative may have been something beyond press coverage or sales of his future book and movie—possibly a desire for a greater good.

Gallup's Clifton also shared an introspective view on the state of the US educational system similar to the one I heard Bill Gates give to the National Conference of State Legislatures in 2005. Clifton drew a picture of the US educational system that can line up 100 kindergarten-age kids and identify those with the greatest athletic potential and provide them with opportunities, coaches, and mentors who will instill in them the skills to excel. This system continues into their teen and young adult years, which is one of the reasons the United States consistently produces more great athletes across a broader spectrum of sport disciplines than any other society. This system can also line up that same 100 kids and identify those with the greatest academic potential and turn them into some of the world's top scientists, mathematicians, accountants, and engineers. Clifton, like Gates, said that despite these attributes, the United States falls short in identifying the best entrepreneurial minds, problem solvers, and innovators. Independent thought, critical thinking, out-of-the-box mindsets, entrepreneurship, innovation, and creativity are needed more than ever in today's competitive world.

In the future, our educational systems must be integral to the development of deeper levels of thinking, problem-solving, and awareness. Nowhere will this be more important than on natural resource and environmental issues.

Global responsibility

Thinking locally and acting globally can be an integral part of future educational systems not just in the United States but around the globe. In future generations, for problem solvers to outnumber problem creators, education must foster that independent thinking and must shift away from follow-the-herd mindsets. In order to remain relevant and compete in the future, successful educational institutions must evolve to become incubators of this mindset. A growing number already are, finding new ways to teach because their students are catalysts for change, pushing old-generation teachers to adapt and evolve or be left behind.

I saw this firsthand during one of my daughter's new-student college orientations, when a professor at Colorado State University was explaining school policies on cell phone and electronic device usage in classrooms and lecture halls. For several years, the institution had tried banning them from classrooms, but she said that, eventually, university leaders acknowledged that smartphones and electronic devices have become so prevalent in modern society that banning them was a lost cause. Yet, over time, it turned out the lost cause was not the students but the old-school approach of the educational institution itself.

Once Colorado State's administration gave up on the electronics ban, she said, it quickly became common in her lectures and classes for many of the students to have their smartphones and tablets out. They weren't texting each other about their evening plans, but, instead, most were on the Internet—fact-checking what was being presented in the lectures. And if the students found contradictory research or information online, they raised their hands and asked her tougher questions. As the CSU professor said, "They keep me on my toes, constantly pushing me to improve."

I heard a similar message from Quest University president David Helfand in 2012. Welcoming its first students in 2007 in the rainforest of British Columbia, Canada, Quest built its academic system from a blank slate, from the ground up. Rather than sticking with the outmoded insular educational system of most universities around the globe, which traces back to the Prussian system *Rich Dad Poor Dad* author Robert Kiyosaki says was designed several hundred years ago to create soldiers who would follow rather than entrepreneurs who would question, Quest's founders asked, "How can we do this differently?" How could they foster more creativity, innovation, and problem-solving?

Quest's founders developed an educational structure without a structure. There are no huge lecture halls with professors giving the same lectures year after year to students who are supposed to take notes, then be assessed on their ability to memorize and regurgitate them back. Instead, Quest has no "professors" at all, only "tutors," who facilitate student learning in rooms containing oval conference tables, where everyone is equal (including the tutors). No more lectures from podiums to students in symmetrical rows in windowless lecture halls, acting as scribes. Instead, they encourage students whose problem-solving, critical thinking, and innovation skills are fostered by action.

During a Quest parent and prospective student visit, I experienced firsthand a very different educational environment than my own 30 years earlier. That day at Quest, parents were divided into groups of 19 or fewer, just as the students are during the regular academic year, to participate in simulated class sessions. It began with the tutor breaking us down into smaller groups of four to five and giving each group information on a fox breeding program in Russia in the 1950s, along with some questions for us to consider. In those small groups, we were asked to discuss and debate those questions and then make a presentation on our findings to the entire class.

An hour later, as each group presented its findings, the room filled with laughter, curiosity, and energy. We all acted more like teenagers than serious adults. In the course of the presentations and ensuing group discussion, the tutor pointed out that, in less than an hour, we had all just tested, understood, and then presented the key elements of Darwin's theory of evolution to our fellow classmates. It was not based on a lecture or PowerPoint from a professor at a podium but on exploring, understanding, and talking through the multiyear experiments ourselves. Based on this approach, the students at this small school who graduated in its first class in 2011 have already made breakthrough discoveries in fields such as mathematics. They are part of a wave of educational discovery that is cresting at Quest and may be the tip of the proverbial iceberg on educational change.[1]

Possibilities are made endless at Quest, largely because the students are encouraged to get out of the classroom, leave the campus itself, and pursue their interests. Quest does this by following the block system pioneered by Colorado College and other schools who are shaking things up. Under the block system, students take just one subject at a time for several weeks, complete that course, and then move on to the next subject. This allows groups studying geology to get out in the mountains with picks and shovels and chip away at rocks themselves rather than examine samples in a classroom or lab. Those studying environmental sciences get out into watersheds, forests, and the nearby ocean. As Helfand said to our parent gathering, "In a world where anyone can get the answer to any question on the Internet in less than five minutes, the educational system needs to evolve."

Just as Al Gore facilitated the development of the Internet and got Exxon and Shell into Russia out of a desire for the greater good, Quest University was founded not by a government grand plan or someone looking for financial gain but by a combined team of educators looking to change the system and philanthropists looking to give something back. Quest's founding donors made their fortunes in businesses like mining and trade. These donors wanted to use their wealth to make the pie bigger for future generations by fostering innovation and creativity.

In the future, leading schools who teach global environmental responsibility and stewardship rather than advocacy curriculums can foster a new generation of critical thinkers, environmental entrepreneurs, and problem solvers. In doing so, they will likely attract the highest achieving, most entrepreneurial minds from around the globe, and those high achievers will become future world leaders in healthcare, education, government, and society.

Moving out of blaming and into problem-solving

In our individual lives, we must move out of blaming governments, corporations, environmental groups, or fate for our problems and into problem-solving and cooperation. We must replace our guilt-based mindsets with positive, hopeful visions of the future.

In the early chapters of this book, I examined how interest groups and politicians have too often fallen into us-versus-them approaches, instigating herd thinkers to stampede. Identifying those unconstructive approaches is important for understanding how those approaches hold us back. The point is not to vilify or scapegoat but, instead, to shift the focus away from what is not working and toward what is.

Our future society can move toward cooperation, like Quest University parents testing and understanding Darwin's theory of evolution. That approach can lead to ever more breakthroughs in science, technology, health, environmental, and natural resource development issues. Along the way, perceived crises like "peak oil" will be solved not through a minimalist, sky-is-falling scarcity mindset but through an approach based on innovation and abundance, with a what-is-possible, glass-half-full mindset. Educational systems and institutions that instill this moving forward will lead rather than be left behind and will build the educational foundation for an ever-improving society.

10

Improving the Environment through a Better Society and Leadership

Moving into the future, environmental policies and natural resource projects should be evaluated on what they can do to improve the local and global situation, compared with realistic potential alternatives around the globe. When new oil and gas or water pipelines, mines, landfills, solar panels and windmill farms and inner-city housing projects are proposed, we need to evaluate how solid their environmental plans and project designs are rather than continuing the current situation where too many decisions are made based on who prints the catchiest bumper-sticker slogans. We should all go a step further to consider whether and how proposed projects can be done in an environmentally sound fashion and spearhead the creation of high-quality jobs and sustainable economic growth.

As legitimate issues arise, we should ask if and how projects can be improved, rather than falling into old all-or-nothing thinking. I saw this happen on the routing for offshore pipelines for the multibillion-dollar Shell Sakhalin-II project in Russia. When questions were raised about Shell's proposed undersea route through an important feeding habitat of critically endangered Pacific gray whales, questions arose, and Shell had their own environmental scientists and third-party experts engage with government regulatory agencies, local and regional administrations, international financing institutions, and local and international environmental groups. In 2005, this collective effort resulted in changes to the pipeline routing in a timely and rational fashion, which resulted in a project being improved through collective engagement, with people sitting around the table and working together rather than just pointing fingers at each other. In the process, over several years Shell funded extensive biological studies on the whales' feeding and migration patterns, which advanced scientific understanding of the species.

When pipeline projects like Keystone are proposed, society needs to move to a place where questions and concerns are considered in a global context that includes looking at potential design and route improvements, not just *Stop it now* or *Drill, baby, drill* perspectives.

In Keystone's case, this would have meant a middle ground between a do-nothing paralysis and a do-it-now approach and looking objectively at questions such as whether the pipeline route and design could be improved like Shell did in Sakhalin. Worth examining, for instance: Is moving crude oil by railroad tank cars across the country better than by pipeline? And if the current rail infrastructure could not handle the increased traffic, would that lead to increased truck transportation on highways and interstates? If so, what would be the safety and air quality implications of this increased truck traffic?

As new solid waste facilities—garbage dumps—are proposed in growing communities, we should ask about their design standards, environmental impacts, regulatory reviews, and plans for the sites once the landfills are full. In Alaska's largest city, when our old city dump filled up and was closed over 30 years ago, a park with softball diamonds and soccer fields was built on top of it. The emerging Javier de la Vega Park became a community asset, with sports facilities that have been in use for decades now, avoiding the need to clear forestland or fill in wetlands someplace else. This is part of a nationwide trend: Thousands of trash dumps across the country have been converted into parks and recreational facilities. Many of them predate our current environmental and zoning laws, going back as far as 1910, when Chicago's Comiskey Park was built on an old city dump. Comiskey was followed by Denver's Mile High Stadium, built on a former trash dump in 1948, and Giants Stadium in New Jersey.[1] The 1976 opening of Giants Stadium and the associated Meadowlands Sports Complex on the site of former trash dumps and industrial plants came out of a more formal process when the New Jersey legislature created the Hackensack Meadowlands Development Commission in 1968 to address both economic and environmental issues concerning the Meadowlands wetlands. This trend toward a formalized process for determining future uses for old trash dumps is described in the EPA's *Closed Waste Sites as Community Assets* report.[2]

Most of us are probably unaware of these highly visible examples, just like many other less prominent former trash dumps that have been converted into green spaces, sports fields, and parklands under the process the EPA describes for turning "closed waste sites into community assets." This is an example of what agencies like the EPA should be doing in regard to sharing constructive and helpful information to society, unlike their negative press release spin I described earlier.

All of this is not to say that we should generate more trash but, rather, that we should look at what is possible when communities have the wealth and ingenuity to turn these liabilities into assets. Thinking back on the trash-laden roadsides and Caribbean beaches of Belize City, I can only imagine how different that all would be if Belize had the human drive and economic means to clean up all those plastic bags and bottles, tires, and oil cans and put them into a modern trash facility that would eventually be converted into a new city park or sports facility.

This same reality applies to the reclamation of old mines and rock quarries. The 2015 US Open golf tournament was played at the now famous Chambers Bay Golf Course, near Tacoma, Washington. Overlooking Puget Sound, this beautifully designed course was built on the site of an old rock quarry that I remember passing many times as a child riding the train. Use of the rock quarry site dated as far back as the Steilacoom Indian tribe and the first European settlers in 1832. Over the past century, it was also the location of a paper mill, a major industrial center, multiple lumber mills, a railroad center, a bus barn, and a regional wastewater treatment plant. Today, it is a preservation and public recreation area with miles of trails through restored and enhanced wildlife habitat, government offices for the local county, and that world-class championship golf course. Site of the nation's largest sand and gravel producer in the 1990s, it transformed in less than 15 years from mineral extraction and resource industry site to city park.[3]

When projects like new wind farms are proposed, we should look at their total impact, including the power lines to transport the electricity they generate into existing electrical grids. In Alaska, when the Cook Inlet Region Native corporation spearheaded construction of the Fire Island Wind Project on an island adjacent to Alaska's largest city, getting the electricity generated by that wind farm into the city's existing electrical grid involved burying cables under expansive tidal flats of a bay where iconic beluga whales were being considered for listing on the endangered species list, past a city park and airport, along a popular bike trail, and then into the existing power grid. The process of evaluating the project worked. As it moved ahead, construction of the buried transmission line took a matter of months, and, just a year later, it was virtually impossible to tell where the cables had been buried.

When local groups and powerful politicians organize to oppose wind power projects based on aesthetics off the coasts of Cape Cod, Martha's Vineyard, and Nantucket Island, and the Scottish wind farm Donald Trump opposed due to the visual impact on his own golf real estate development, we need these projects to be evaluated in an unbiased process with neutral referees. This process should also consider the impact of producing the steel, copper, molybdenum, and concrete needed for the wind farms compared with the alternatives, including where these materials will come from.

Under a "think locally, act globally" perspective, when new mines are proposed, they should be evaluated on thorough environmental studies, engineering designs, and considerations like water quality in an unbiased process where everyone considers the viable alternatives around the globe. When a mine like the Rosemont Copper project outside of Tucson, Arizona, is proposed, we should all consider the alternative of producing the copper for our smartphones, refrigerators, and hybrid cars from an EPA-regulated mine in Arizona versus those in other places around the world (with attention, too, to their respective environmental stewardship standards).

The end of bumper-sticker politicians

In the increasingly dysfunctional US political arena, local, state, and national leaders too often migrate to the extremes of worst-case and best-case scenarios. When politicians oversimplify complicated issues with bumper-sticker rhetoric, we should rise up and tell them it's not acceptable, regardless of whether it is *Drill here; drill now* Newt Gingrich rhetoric or Barbara Boxer fearmongering ("The pipeline project will increase the price of gas, while the tar sands flowing through the pipeline will result in pollution that causes serious illnesses like asthma and increases in carbon pollution").

As we insist that leaders and government regulators consider all cases, including complicated middle grounds, we will encourage more innovation and creativity. The result will be better options for the global environment and society as a whole. Rather than following the emotions of groups who can scream the loudest, we need a process in which we consider facts and data. This could ultimately lead to better projects, such as one in Playa del Rey, California, in the heart of both prime Los Angeles real estate and coastal wetlands. On the site of an abandoned Hughes Aircraft manufacturing plant and runway, an industrial blight was transformed into beautiful, high-quality multistory living communities. Playa del Rey was built with European-feeling central parks that meld playgrounds and green spaces with wetland enhancement; these communities are lined by cafés and small shops, sports fields, a new school, and modern office buildings.

Better regulators

We need regulators who are impartial referees rather than cheerleaders. Government regulators must become more accountable moving forward as impartial problem solvers, who employ common sense and a global perspective that doesn't lose the forest through the trees. Too often, in today's world, environmental regulators fall into acting like cheerleaders, like the EPA in recent years when it issued more press releases each month than all of the major oil companies combined or when it gets caught in abstract, tabletop interpretations of laws and regulations. These interpretations are too often developed in government office buildings and cubicles and too often lack common sense, forcing the expenditure of huge amounts of money for marginal benefit to the environment and directing critical financial resources away from projects with potentially greater environmental and public good. By working atop the foundations of the National Environmental Policy Act, the Clean Air Act, the Clean Water Act, and related frameworks, laws, and regulations, regulatory agencies need to set high bars for projects based on facts and science and to enforce those consistently and impartially and with common sense.

These same agencies, starting with the EPA, need to close down their press release machines. Instead, we should insist that they post decisions, rulings, and comments on proposed projects and permits online on easily accessible public websites in a fully transparent fashion for all to see. Just like leaders in Greenland and students at schools like Quest University, we are smart enough to interpret things ourselves, rather than relying on news media accounts of major regulatory agency decisions that are based on press releases spoon-fed from those agencies' PR people.

We need a system where government regulatory decisions and the underlying rationale for decisions are publicly posted online, in an unbiased and factual fashion, for all to see. While many government agencies are moving in this direction already, they still, unfortunately, cherry-pick what is posted. Interior Secretary Sally Jewell's Bureau of Land Management undertook a time-intensive and costly process to develop a long-term strategy for potential oil and gas development in the National Petroleum Reserve in Alaska's Arctic. This area was designated by Congress for energy development decades ago and is now being carefully explored by energy companies using the latest in modern technology with Department of the Interior oversight to ensure strong environmental stewardship. In the process, public comments sought by the Department of the Interior (DOI) were posted online on a US government website. But rather than being open and transparent, government regulators who were supposed to be impartial referees selectively posted comments in 2016 that suited their cheerleader-like agenda. And they decided not to post on their website a comment letter by the Arctic Slope Regional Corporation, a group that represents thousands of Iñupiat Eskimo shareholders who live in the region; they said it was not "relevant," potentially because it laid out a reasonable basis for more energy development than the regulators supported. Yet on the website that described the planning effort, those same regulators prominently posted a document from 1979 that was more suited to the regulators' less-is-better approach to energy development in the area. This document, by its very nature, did not consider improvements in environmental protection and energy development technology over the past 40 years.[4]

John Hofmeister of Citizens for Affordable Energy has proposed depoliticizing who our regulators ultimately answer to. Nearly a hundred years ago, the banking system was separated into the Federal Reserve Board and chairman, who have staggered terms and don't answer to politicians in Congress or the president, and Hofmeister says we need a similar approach to natural resource decisions. That Federal Reserve System is designed to immunize impartial financial regulatory decisions from the political agendas of sitting presidents like Donald Trump and Barack Obama and congressional political agendas of the likes of Barbara Boxer and Ted Cruz. The time has come for an independent system like the Federal Reserve for handling natural resource regulatory decisions.

Charged with protecting environmental health, regulators have more tools, technology, and resources at their disposal than ever. With these resources and modern technology, today's regulators should also have more common sense, independence, and commitment to informing and educating the public fairly and responsibly as expert referees, rather than cheerleading and scapegoating.

The EPA's budget and workforce

With an $8 billion annual budget and over 15,000 employees, government regulators at agencies like the EPA have substantial resources at their disposal,[5] and they should have state-of-the-art systems in place to take decisive action on environmental issues and project permits.

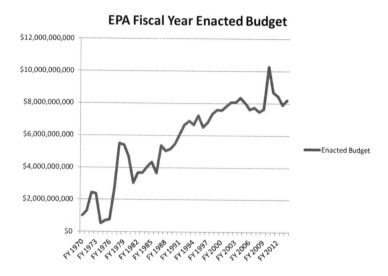

In the area of human health, the Food and Drug Administration, often subject to complaints about their bureaucratic delays in approving new breakthrough vaccines, set an example in moving decisively to protect human health in 2016 with their ruling on the health impacts of the new e-cigarette vaping fad. Not so long ago, in the case of tobacco cigarettes, it took decades for US public health regulators to confirm definitively that smoking tobacco products caused fatal lung cancer and heart disease. In our parents' generation, it was not uncommon for family doctors to smoke, even in their offices. Over time, research and science proved what many had suspected for years: Cigarettes were killing people at astronomical rates. Back then, it took decades for the federal government to make that official determination and even longer for public places, restaurants, offices, and once smoke-filled airplanes to go smoke free (efforts I have been involved with since 1996).

Contrast that with the recent proliferation of e-cigarette vaping. Originally touted by tobacco interests a few short years ago as tools designed to help adults quit smoking, e-cigarettes are, in reality, branded, packaged, and targeted at children, encouraging kids to start using them through sophisticated tactics such as cotton candy and bubblegum flavors. These products are often placed in retail store display cases at heights more visible to children than to adults, much like sugary cereals in grocery stores. As vaping quickly spread across the country, including in no-smoking sections of public places like airports and even airplanes, research concluded within a few short years that vaping e-cigarettes was a major health hazard, and they were declared subject to FDA regulation—with the associated public health safeguards.

This is a prime example of human innovation with negative health consequences and sophisticated marketing by big businesses running into a strong regulatory process that was able to take decisive action based on research for the protection of everyone's health by preserving our ability to breathe clean air. In many places, the air today is less polluted from cigarettes, factory smokestacks, and car exhaust than just 20 years ago.

Activist groups pitch in

Environmental groups, who have quietly emerged as one of the largest special interest contributors to political campaigns in recent years, should end their tactic of bankrolling election campaigns of their favored politicians. Instead, they should put their super PAC dollars to work advancing scientific research and pitch in more collaboratively to efforts that will bring real change to the world based on facts and collaborative science rather than protests, bumper-sticker slogans, lawsuits, and political contributions.

In advancing the common good, activist groups should take a more meaningful approach, asking, "What are we for, and how can we collaborate?" Those supporting them in the societal grandstand should insist that environmental activist groups pitch in rather than throw inside pitches. Society should ask tough questions of third-party activist groups who engage in us-versus-them hustles on projects and issues without engaging in consideration of potential improvements and alternatives.

In the future, efforts by conservation groups to partner with mining companies, like The Nature Conservancy did with Rio Tinto on the design of a mine in Mongolia, should become the rule rather than the exception. Activist groups should operate at standards held high by their members and donors, the news media, politicians, regulatory agencies, and businesses as we all consider individual projects and environmental issues from a global perspective.

Better media

Following in the steps of Quest University students, the media should go beyond traditional cut-and-paste us-versus-them story angles and end the associated overuse of the same quotable sources again and again to produce predictable headlines. We must insist that the media be impartial and look at best- and not just worst-case scenarios and the often even more complicated middle ground on natural resource and environmental issues. If we insist on this, the media will have no option but to become better at independently analyzing issues of the day rather than simply regurgitating spoon-fed messages from businesses, politicians, regulators, and activist group press releases.

This is a call to action for a much-needed policy environment where educational, public health, economic, and natural resource issues and projects are evaluated on what they can do to improve the local and global situation in the context of realistic potential alternatives around the globe, where the not-in-my-backyard syndrome becomes the exception rather than the rule.

11

A New Path for Big Business

My experience working in Russia starting in the late 1990s led to meeting some of the world's most highly educated and underutilized people, including many with PhDs in technical fields like the natural sciences and mathematics. It struck me also that Russia had a chronic shortage of entrepreneurs. An exception was a small group of Russian computer whizzes at a software company. They and the other small Russian companies they teamed with had undertaken innovative projects such as developing and deploying commercial voice over Internet protocol (VOIP) calling for individuals before Skype was even invented. They also wrote sophisticated software programs for commodities and options traders in the United States. I reflected on this when seeing men of the same age as those Russian programmers in Madagascar, 15 years later, still trading chickens for bananas.

As the global human population continues to increase, a new world order for business can emerge in which businesses and corporations become the most important vehicles for change around natural resource stewardship, use, and conservation.

Vast numbers of people around the globe are transitioning out of poverty. As they move up Maslow's hierarchy of needs, we need to find new ways to maximize the efficiency of natural resource use and ensure strong environmental stewardship. As Maslow hypothesized nearly 100 years ago, people moving out of poverty will want more than just their daily food, heat, and shelter needs met. Today, that means they will demand more and more modern healthcare and medicine; transportation; higher-quality food; better education; social, artistic, and creative opportunities; and entrepreneurial and business opportunities as they move beyond just living hand to mouth.

As huge numbers of people move away from basic economies that trade bananas for chickens, they will want to move away from individual subsistence mining, logging, and fishing and into opportunities including higher-paying modern mining and energy-related jobs. The Red Dog mine in the remote Arctic of Alaska is a case study in what is possible in this transition. At Red Dog, the majority of the workers are Alaska Natives who average over $100,000 per year in pay and have full health and retirement benefits as they mine the zinc that UNICEF and the Clinton Foundation are deploying to stop the tragedy of childhood diarrhea in India, Africa, and South America.

People will have more wealth and greater purchasing power as they move up Maslow's hierarchy, as is already happening in Chile, Brazil, Colombia, and South Africa. As consumers in places like these around the globe have more wealth and purchasing power, more will have the financial resources to demand a better path for the businesses and corporations who supply their needs.

To drive this change, we as informed consumers must move away from supporting companies who try to out-green each other to win popularity contests in order to increase their sales and, instead, spend our money to support businesses pursuing true global environmental responsibility and innovation. This means moving away from blindly buying products just because they put *Please recycle* on their plastic packaging, questioning the true environmental footprint of their supply chain, and asking companies like Apple where the components for their renewable-powered plant in Prineville, Oregon, are actually mined and smelted. It means holding high-end jewelers accountable for more details when they sign on to "No dirty gold" campaigns while telling US financial regulators they can't tell where the gold in their jewelry comes from.[1] With outdoor equipment companies who oppose mining, even though virtually everything they make and sell is derived from mining and oil products, it means asking them tough questions and supporting businesses that pay real, meaningful attention to where the stuff inside their products comes from.[2] It means directing our purchases toward companies who have truly sustainable supply chains around the world that supply the products and services we need in the most economic, environmentally efficient, and innovative ways possible, whether we live in elite supercities like New York, London, or Seattle or in remote third- and fourth-world countries.

New supply chains are critical to fostering improvements in things such as how to move crops from fields where they are harvested in places like Africa and Chile to huge population centers. Greater efficiency in that supply chain means far less spoilage and loss in transportation and lower costs as people move away from hauling harvests by Zebu cattle carts toward faster, more efficient means. Innovations are already unfolding, spearheaded by business research by previously vilified companies like Monsanto who can produce better-quality food for cities in Africa and South America by raising crops that require less water and have higher yields, lower prices, and produce higher value for farmers. Already, farmers in Africa are increasingly using text messages to keep in contact with those who sell the food they produce in city markets and are thus better able to manage the timing of their production. Businesses in places like this who participate in this change will thrive—and as they do, companies and entrepreneurs we haven't even heard of yet will become the next generation's Bill Gates.

Catalysts for these changes will also include companies like new-school electric car manufacturer Tesla and old-school defense contractors like Lockheed Martin. Tesla is leading the charge to go a step beyond Apple and engaging in the actual supply sourcing of metals and materials for their plants and products, including the graphite for their car batteries. While companies like Tesla are shaking up the automobile world, Lockheed Martin may be a catalyst for shaking up the aviation world as they invest significant sums of time, money, and effort to combine old blimp technology with modern aviation lift design for a potential wave of the aviation future: commercial airships that could move people and freight with less energy and lower costs than airplanes. And Tesla and Lockheed Martin could be the tip of the iceberg.

As billions of people move out of poverty around the globe and their purchasing power increases, we will see economic activity at levels we and our parents likely never imagined—and with the advent of the Internet and smartphones, consumers are more informed than ever. This new generation of consumers will ask companies like Apple where the nickel in the batteries for their iPhones comes from, where the materials for hybrid and electric cars come from, and they won't stop there. This new generation of consumers will ask where the electricity comes from that recharges these electric cars when they plug them into their home wall outlets or the growing networks of recharging stations being deployed by Tesla, car manufacturers in Europe, and even electric utilities themselves in the United States.

Companies who don't just react but proactively anticipate these changes will find new markets—and thrive. Static businesses who don't adapt will be left behind in their wake—leaving many household names to go the way of the payphone, black-and-white TV, eight-track player, and floppy disk. Many of these likely successful future companies have been successful adapters and innovators for generations. Long-established innovators like ExxonMobil, Shell, BP, and General Electric may be who bring this future to reality as they find and implement new breakthrough and disruptive technologies and products. While companies like Uber and Tesla put energy and resource efficiency into practice in answering the demands of more and more highly informed consumers.

Even oil companies have not been exempt from the societal push for companies to "green" their goods—or at least appear to do so. ExxonMobil has been one of the world's most methodical, slow-to-change, bureaucratic organizations; it is also one of the world's most successful, due largely to its disciplined approach to decision-making. As a result, ExxonMobil was one of the last oil companies to embark on a campaign to position itself and its products as green, despite consistently being one of the world's largest investors in technological breakthroughs and innovation around energy production and use. Following an approach similar to that described in *Superforecasting* by Philip Tetlock and Don Gardner, ExxonMobil went outside its own cul-de-sac over the course of several years, engaged with other global players with diverse views like the United Nations Council on Climate Change, and invested in partnerships with Stanford University in undertaking a data-driven analysis of the underlying issues. Yet this story was not picked up by big media in the world of oversimplified us-versus-them coverage of environmental issues.

The rapid success of these businesses will breed even more innovation. Major oil companies are some of the world's biggest investors in new, energy-efficient technologies. With growing markets, they will do ever more of that and will talk more openly about it as several major oil companies did in 2017. In future decades, due to increased energy efficiency and greater use of new technologies like electric cars, it will be the adaptable energy producers, refiners, and distributors who will thrive, while those who rest on their laurels will be left behind. While the *leave it in the ground* movement uses oversimplified bumper-sticker reasoning to say we should stop producing oil and gas, the opposite is actually true. Oil and gas will remain a critical leg to the future higher-efficiency, high-innovation economy as many experts forecast dramatic growth in things like deployment of more electric cars. The energy to power them will come from somewhere.

Former president Obama said during his Arctic visit to Alaska in 2015, "Oil is a bridge fuel." It will be the legacy energy companies with the economic means from their success who make fossil fuels last longer than even they may imagine. Along the way, they will invent technologies that are ever more efficient in energy production, distribution, and utilization to supply a global population of people moving up Maslow's hierarchy of needs. Using the success and know-how from smart, environmentally responsible, and efficient current and future operations, mining companies will continue to find new ways to mine and more efficiently produce the zinc needed to address childhood diarrhea in poor countries; the rare earth metals needed for medical equipment; and the metals needed for high-tech educational institutions and systems, smartphones, and modern lightweight high-fuel-mileage cars. Using money earned from successful projects, they will fund breakthroughs in new ways to produce these metals that will make places like China's Baotou environmental Armageddon a thing of the past. A new generation of political leaders will look increasingly at *real* meaningful environmental stewardship as a core value, rather than a bumper sticker slogan.

12

Improve Humanity

A key lesson from my work advocating for funding for Alaskan teen suicide prevention and my service work for the National Organization for Prevention of Child Abuse and Neglect (NOPCAN) in Belize was the importance of hope, opportunity, and connection for young people, with mentors and positive role models. For young people in Alaska Native villages in the North and in the Central American mangroves and rainforests of Belize, hope for the future is bleak when there is no one to look up to. When communities unravel, as has happened too often in both places, young people suffer increasing tolls of neglect, abuse, the ills of alcohol and drug problems, and tragically high rates of obesity-related diseases such as diabetes.

When communities are in downward spirals, teen suicide rates often increase, and the cycle of tragedy continues. The biggest problem many of these communities face is the growing numbers of young people walking around their villages and communities staring at their shoelaces. They have little reason to pursue higher education, college studies, or even a high school diploma when there are virtually no opportunities to put them to use. In much of rural Alaska, this generation of young people often face a world with employment opportunities limited to a few weeks of fishing in the summer and virtually no jobs during the other ten months of the year.

A Gallup poll, which CEO Jim Clifton said "tracked the will of the world for ten years," found that "what everyone in the world wants is a good job." This is a sociological finding of great significance: "People want a good job; they don't want informal jobs or self-employment out of necessity." Gallup's analytics showed that "of the 7 billion people in the world, there are 5 billion adults aged 15 and older. Of these 5 billion, 3 billion of them . . . desire a full-time job. Only 1.3 billion actually have a good job, which means that the real unemployment rate in the world is over 50 percent."[1] In fact, they want a good job even more than a clean environment, better public health, world peace, or any number of other important things. When it comes to those who are unemployed and underemployed, when there is no hope for the brighter future that those billions of people aspire after, social ills increase correspondingly.

There is hope for turning this around. It starts with greater employment opportunities for young people, and it means giving people a reason to pursue higher education. When youth have more hope, they have more reasons to get up in the morning when the alarm goes off. They have more reason to stay clean and sober and pursue an education.

As Gallup found, protecting the environment and other important priorities are secondary for the chronically un- and underemployed. Yet when we protect and improve the global environment, we can directly and profoundly improve things for humanity itself. When people have high-quality jobs and opportunities, they take greater pride in their communities, homes, and environments; walk with more of a bounce in their step; and start looking others in the eye, and the rates of teen suicide, child abuse, and obesity decline.

When this happens, there can be more wealth to afford greater environmental stewardship.

As people and communities become truly economically empowered, changes occur like those I witnessed firsthand during my five years working on projects in the Russian Far East capital city of Yuzhno-Sakhalinsk on Sakhalin Island, as I've discussed previously. In the mid-1990s, Yuzhno- Sakhalinsk was a bleak Soviet-era planned city filled with drab deteriorating gray cement apartment buildings, trash everywhere, weeds overgrowing city parks and the planned green spaces of main boulevards, and apartment courtyards filled with trash and dog excrement. Then, corresponding with the infusion of investment capital from ExxonMobil and Shell's multi-billion-dollar international oil and gas projects in the region, things started to turn around. Yuzhno-Sakhalinsk made the shift as city parks were cleaned up, the grass in public places was mown regularly, flowers were planted in public spaces, trash-lined streets were cleaned up, and apartment and office buildings increasingly sprung new siding and paint.

Yuzhno-Sakhalinsk was as dreary and depressing as any place else in the world in the mid-1990s, before those billions of dollars in international oil and gas investment began to flow. Those investments fueled a great turnaround for the vast region—so much so that that region, which had been a laggard even by Russian standards, completely reversed course. In the process, it became a highly desired destination for Russians seeking more economic, social, and societal opportunity. It has become a diamond among Russia's rough broader economic and population declines over those same 15 years, and in the process, young people in Yuzhno-Sakhalinsk now hope for a better future than previous generations. The increased abundance of good-quality, intellectually challenging jobs with upward mobility created by this oil and gas development also spurred environmental improvements, with the capital city finally having the resources and willpower to extinguish a fire and smoky haze that had been smoldering in the city's trash dump for years.

We all want hope

We all want to help humanity and protect the environment for the good of human health and the good of the planet and threatened species. Unfortunately, too often those who care the most are susceptible to missing the big picture of how the environment itself can be better protected and stewarded when there is more wealth to afford to do the right things. We all must not lose the big picture of *why*: The good of the global environment is for the good of all human health and that of other species, not just in our backyards. Environmentally well-stewarded natural resource projects can be the bridge to a better future, especially when we take a global view and pitch in to ensure that projects use the best modern science and technology and know-how and take advantage of human ingenuity. We can learn from the environmental mistakes of the past, such as the legacy of decades of Soviet-era pollution from unstewarded oil development, the *Exxon Valdez* oil spill, pollution at communist-era mines in Romania, and the Mount Polley mine tailings dam failure in Canada in 2014. Energy and minerals projects can energize economies and societies like those in bush Alaska, Belize, and the Russian Far East while protecting the environment at the same time.

Investments in responsible resource projects can and will provide the means for vast improvements in living conditions around the globe. And these improvements will be more meaningful and more sustainable than just coin donation jars next to the cash registers at our local cafés.

With investment, the conditions can be improved. Un- and under-employment can decrease or potentially be eliminated—as Iceland has shown, cutting teen drinking and drug use from the highest in Europe to the lowest in just a decade while doubling University enrollment. Iceland did that through economic development that centered on responsible use of their energy resource wealth. The rest of the world can use Iceland's example as a starting point rather than a finish line.

Poverty can be addressed in African countries like Madagascar and in other places around the globe while environmental quality is improved as trash is cleaned up, like in Yuzhno-Sakhalinsk. Far fewer people will be forced to cook and heat their homes with charcoal in places like Madagascar, which could reverse one of the underlying drivers behind deforestation. Silt fills streams in parts of Madagascar due to that deforestation and subsistence farming as millions of people live hand to mouth. Natural gas development in the adjacent Mozambique Channel by international oil companies is leading to a stronger economy there, and the people of Madagascar could eventually shift away from meager rural to more modern communities, allowing the jungle to regenerate. With similar development, nearby Kenya doubled the number of people connected to the electric grid in just the three years from 2013 to 2016. Now, 55 percent of the population is on the electric grid.[2]

As all of this unfolds, there are huge opportunities for improvement in other important areas like women's health and child labor rights, two things that many in the developed world consider inalienable rights but, unfortunately, are nothing more than a dream to many in less developed regions. Improvements in these areas are connected to having more responsible economic development in places with third- and fourth-world conditions, not less.

As *The Intelligent Optimist* (then published as *Ode for Intelligent Optimists*) magazine wrote in a series of articles on menopause in

2012, there are benefits of new approaches, including diets high in omega-3 vitamins and more yoga for women.[3] While that all probably sounded fine to most of the magazine's readers in developed countries like Holland, Singapore, Canada, and the United States, it might seem like a stretch to even think of this as realistic for many women in third- and fourth-world countries.

But not so fast. If we look back at the rapid development and increased standards of living many places around the world have experienced in our lifetimes, maybe it is possible. Women living in places like Madagascar can hope to move up Maslow's hierarchy and have access to omega-3 vitamin supplements and yoga mats not from government handouts from afar but through rapid economic empowerment like what has occurred for those in the Russian Far East Sakhalin Region, Iceland, Chile, Colombia, and Brazil.

With growing economies and modern technology, opportunities can spread to more and more women in third- and fourth-world countries. In the process, young people will have more hope and opportunity, the rates of child abuse and neglect and teen suicide will decrease, and menopause diets high in omega-3 vitamins and yoga practices can be realistic goals. As this unfolds, young people will have more reason to get up in the morning when the alarm goes off, look up rather than staring down at their shoelaces, pursue educations, and have greater hope for a brighter future.

13

The Last Shall Be First

We all have a huge opportunity to help turn poverty around throughout the world. In the process, quantum shifts can empower struggling communities to make game-changing improvements in environmental stewardship and economic progress. In the process, they can transition the lives of people facing some of the harshest economic, environmental, and social challenges around the globe today. People once locked in poverty and desperation, struggling to find the means to feed themselves and their families, can be freed to find prosperity. They can become the leaders who will improve their local environments, providing clean running water and basic sanitation, and increased prosperity will supply the resources to make that happen.

A call to action

Emerging new economic powers like Chile, Brazil, Iceland, and South Africa are moving onto the global stage. Innovation and creativity are thriving in these countries and may lead to breakthroughs many of us can't even imagine today. Indeed, it may be a Pakistani or Russian-born scientist, who has emigrated to escape their stifling home country and is working for an Israeli-funded biotech company in Brazil, who invents the newest cures for the most aggressive forms of cancer or Alzheimer's diseases. Brazil is transforming its economy as it leverages increased economic means from development of its mineral and energy resources to diversify into new fields like biotech. Brazilian science and technology breakthroughs further its economic upward trajectory and provide the economic means to better protect its rainforests, move away from slash-and-burn farming, and better protect endangered species and the Amazon watershed in the process.

Environmental breakthroughs like BioRock, invented at a research institute in Jamaica, may be the cornerstones of new offshore environmental protection approaches for coral reefs around the globe. Places as far away as Australia could use the wealth from their own energy and mineral-driven economy to deploy new BioRock technology for their own reef restoration and enhancement efforts.

Madagascar and other African countries, Greenland, Arctic regions, and Chile's neighbors all have the opportunity to follow in the footsteps of the Chiles of the world. Supply growing global markets with the mineral and energy resources that they need in environmentally responsible ways and use the wealth created by those opportunities to lift up their societies in the process. The same could happen in places like the environmental blights of Baotou, China, and Norilsk, Russia.

To empower this change, the world needs more places where leaders take charge of their own destinies and aren't afraid to take input from global energy and mining companies and environmental activists. Where leaders will decide for themselves whether they can develop their natural resources to the highest global environmental standards. In the unfolding global technological revolution, these political leaders have the opportunity to take a grassroots, bottom-up approach. Entrepreneurs like the one operating the *"Madagascar et ses mines"* café in the Malagasy jungle can be drivers of change that transform the future for "the little guy" in Africa just as visionary Alaska Native leaders believed they could apply modern science and technology to develop Red Dog mine and transform the future of their people in the process.

Conversion from coal fireplaces to natural gas for residential heating led to the dramatic improvements in air quality London experienced when its residents stopped burning coal in their homes following the passage of their own Clean Air Act in 1956 and residents of Los Angeles experienced following America's own Clean Air Act of 1973. Now bustling cities like Antananarivo can improve their air quality as well. To do so, they need the economic means to afford that transition from burning unsustainable wood charcoal gathered from their rapidly denuding forests to the use of natural gas. As emerging countries in Africa and South America use wise development of their natural resources to advance their economies, they can incorporate mass transit and large parks, with bicycle and walking paths, into their urban modernizations from the start. This has been done for generations in Holland—leapfrogging them into the future and avoiding the need for multibillion-dollar retrofits for smarter transit systems like those in North American supercities including Los Angeles, Seattle, and Vancouver.

People in Belize can take advantage of the opportunities I have described in this book to leverage their geographic position, much like Lebanon has done in the Middle East. In the process, Belize could become a regional educational and financial center at the crossroads between South and Central America and North America—potentially a bridge between the growing economies of Brazil, Colombia, Mexico, and the United States. If a country like Lebanon can rebuild itself after a 20-year civil war that left its society in shambles, so can Belize become a regional center of finance and education. Belize and Lebanon are both small, ethnically and religiously diverse countries located between huge natural resource–producing countries and huge consuming countries. Lebanon has leveraged that position to become a financial, educational, and tourism center for commerce and trade, earning it the nickname of the "Switzerland of the Middle East." Belize can follow that path to become the "Switzerland of Central America."

In the 1800s, Britain claimed what is now Belize to have a beachhead in the region as it competed with Spanish and Portuguese explorers. With that claim, it brought the British rule of law, civil society, and eventually the British educational system. Belize first became an official English crown colony in 1862, and since that time has operated under a constitutional system with long-standing representational government, including a ministerial system when it became a territory beginning in 1964, before its eventual independence in 1981. Despite its downward spiral since then, Belize has an educated population, with three-fourths of primary school students going on to secondary schools and an adult literacy rate over 80 percent. It has multiple functioning commercial banks and the academic foundation to become a regional finance power. With its geographic position, it could become a global leader in manufacturing small, energy-efficient affordable homes made of high-efficiency materials, like a young entrepreneur I met there envisioned. This housing could be designed and fabricated in Belize, exported around the world, and help transform stagnant Belize into a leader in sustainable manufacturing. This could pave the way for the construction of new, energy-efficient homes, apartment buildings, and offices needed with the ongoing development of new supercities around the world. It could dramatically improve Belize's overall energy efficiency and also its environmental footprint. Yet that energy-efficient housing requires more materials like copper and other metals than a traditional cinder block home, and therein lies an even bigger opportunity to source the materials for more energy-efficient living from places with the highest environmental and social standards.

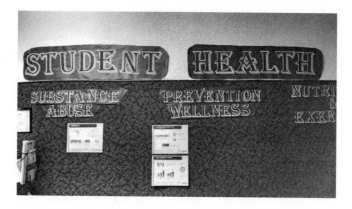

Author photo

Following a similar path, American Indian tribes who face some of the gravest economic and environmental conditions of anyone in the "developed" or undeveloped world can follow in the footsteps of Alaska Native leaders and use their natural resource wealth to lift up their economies and communities while improving their local environments. This approach can provide clean running water and sewer systems for all their residents, improve their educational systems from within, reduce their astronomically high rates of obesity and diabetes, address teenage suicide, and provide young people with greater hope and opportunity for a brighter future. The Redding Rancheria and Hoopa Valley tribes, the Pinoleville Pomo Nation, and the Fort Independence Indian Community in California have taken the initiative themselves to start programs to clean up their communities; remove rusted-out old cars, batteries, trash, and associated junk; and initiate recycling programs.[1] Alaska Native Corporations are also using the wealth created by natural resource development to initiate environmental and recycling programs from the Arctic tundra to coastal rainforests. In the northernmost community in the United States, the Arctic Slope Native Association sponsors the Our Land Community Clean-Up Initiative in an effort to beautify Utqiagvik. This local effort is funded by Native businesses involved in energy development and support-service work and involves neighborhood cleanup, including encouraging proper disposal of wrecked vehicles.

In this local approach to sustainable economic and environmental progress, Greenland's leaders can take the next steps. In the process, they can use the revenue from smart development of their abundant energy and mineral resources to fund world-class fisheries and marine mammal research, improve stewardship of those fisheries and marine mammal resources, and even implement habitat enhancement programs to the benefit of the environment and their residents—for generations to come.

A case study in what can be

"Your project is lifting up an entire region, giving many local people hope for the first time in their lives." These were the first words of a US congressman we ran into one afternoon in 1996 when I was working on the early stages of the Donlin Gold Project. Donlin is an advanced-stage mineral exploration project in the Wade-Hampton area of Southwest Alaska, one of the lowest-income regions in the entire United States. In the ensuing 20-plus years, the international mining companies involved in the project have been working in partnership with two Alaska Native corporations, whose shareholders form most of the population in this region. Donlin is a mineral exploration project similar to the others I have described in remote places where economic opportunity is scarce and social, economic, and community challenges are large.

At Donlin, mining company leaders implemented an aggressive local village hire program from the start to provide much-needed opportunities in villages where jobs were virtually nonexistent and communities had some of the lowest per capita income and highest rates of alcoholism and teen suicide in the United States.

As time went by, many local villagers working on Donlin were better able to buy new aluminum skiffs and snowmobiles, which allowed them to better participate in personal-use subsistence fishing, hunting, and berry picking with the money they earned working their shifts at the mine exploration camp. Young people looked up to them in a region where, in some villages, more than 80 percent of the population received welfare. The region continues to look thoughtfully at this mineral exploration opportunity that could shift its entire economy. The project is being pursued by mining companies with a proven track record of employing local people from communities with challenging conditions and providing them with life skills to prosper in the modern economy, going as far as supporting an Alcoholics Anonymous chapter in their own mining camp.

In Africa, the country of Botswana successfully used its diamond wealth to develop quickly and grew from one of Africa's poorest countries at its independence in 1966 to a democratic, stable, and relatively upper-middle-income country in a short period of time—with associated stronger environmental stewardship. On the same continent, Equatorial Guinea's economy grew an average 17 percent per year between the year 2000 and 2011 due to the development of its resource wealth by international oil companies like ExxonMobil, making it one of the fastest-growing economies in the world and propelling it into the league of higher-income countries, improving the quality of life for countless numbers of its people in the process—truly lifting up those who need it the most.[2]

A new path for all of us

If we as consumers, politicians, media, and regulators from all over the world pay more attention to where the raw materials come from to build new highly energy- and resource-efficient apartment buildings, rail lines, bike corridors—and the bicycles and trains that will use them—we have the opportunity to insist that the materials are from places that apply the highest global technology and environmental standards. In the United States and Europe, Africa, Asia, Greenland, and Central and South America, it means we must have political leaders who acknowledge and celebrate natural resource production successes—rather than hide from them.

The world can look to Northwest Arctic Alaska, Iceland, Botswana, and Equatorial Guinea as examples. Natural resource development and strong environmental stewardship go hand in hand in these countries, providing the means for improved healthcare and education and more opportunities for higher-quality jobs. Their economies are growing, and work conditions, healthcare, education, parks, and recreation opportunities have improved, thanks to government, community, and business leaders committed to doing things right.

We can also improve health conditions in places like the poor West African country of Sierra Leone, which experienced the devastating Ebola outbreak of 2014 that led to thousands of deaths. Sierra Leone could have responded much differently if it had a stronger healthcare system. The most sustainable way to support that better healthcare system and fight off tragedies like that is with a stronger economy.

In the future, those of us around the globe who want to help the little guy can do more than just buy products with *small-scale sustainability* stamped on their packaging. We can look around at the millennials with their smartphones, computer tablets, and carbon bicycles living in ever more energy- and resource-efficient modern apartments and loft condos made of increasing amounts of steel, copper, zinc, molybdenum, and cement, with all of the associated systems running on components made of rare earth metals, and see opportunity. We can invest in the companies producing these materials and spearheading innovation and advancement to lift up entire societies, rather than just doling out pittances from our pocket change.

The end of exploitation

While all these improvements in the areas of environment, economy, education, and healthcare are important, my own experience goes to something deeper.

The scene in the crowded domestic terminal in the African airport of Antananarivo in 2013 reminded me of the chaos of the Tijuana border crossing of the 1980s. Swarms of locals surrounded foreign travelers, insisting on carrying bags for tips or selling them cheap trinkets. Rather than a glitzy, modern airport of the 21st century, Antananarivo's domestic terminal was more like an old, dark 1950s inner-city bus station. On the wall, I saw a small poster that said, *Sex tourism is a crime.* On the turboprop Air Madagascar plane to the remote island of Nosy Be, I noticed an unremarkable elderly Englishman who was flying with a young, striking, very well-dressed African woman. This man was the first of what were clearly many sex tourists I saw on this small African island on the Mozambique Channel.

Walking down the beautiful beach below the small inn where we stayed (which had a *Sex tourism is not allowed here* notice on its website), we walked past other, more ramshackle hotels overlooking the beach. On the verandas, in broad daylight in the middle of the afternoon, we saw numerous elderly white European men laying out, being massaged by young Malagasy girls, many barely teenagers. In the evenings, on the main street behind these hotels, throngs of these young women congregated in the small pubs and cafés in the oceanside village, making eyes at the passing foreign men.

I asked a local French expatriate about the whole scene. He said it was tragic, yet those of us from rich countries needed to understand that in this fourth-world country of 20 million, there is virtually no economy. These young girls face difficult lives, often living with a dozen or more family members in thatched-roof huts, with no schools or other opportunities, where they do laundry in sewage-polluted streams. Yet one evening of sex work could earn them more money than they might make in months trading bananas for chickens. This human tragedy must be turned around, but how?

What if the Obama administration's program advocating for development of Afghanistan's mineral and energy resources to turn that country around by creating 500,000 jobs could be applied to Madagascar as well? What if responsible mining and energy programs could create even 100,000 new jobs in Madagascar?

My own 30-plus years of experience in the energy and mining industries has introduced me to projects, businesses, and places where a huge percentage of professional engineers, geophysicists, geologists, accountants, CFOs, and CEOs are women. What if environmentally responsible development of mineral and energy resources in Madagascar brought these same opportunities? These young teenage girls on the beaches of Nosy Be could be selling the world their expertise in producing mineral and energy products we all need, rather than selling their bodies to feed their families.

14

Better News Media

"We're in a new age of 'yellow journalism'—and it's our job to change that," said the CEO of Alaska Public Media (public broadcasting) when we met over coffee discussing public broadcasting funding that I have advocated for over the past 20-plus years. Public broadcasting is leading the news world toward more information and less sensationalism with programs like *The Solutions Desk*, *The Energy Desk*, and *Indie Alaska*.

The Solutions Desk features community-driven reporting on people and programs solving Alaska's problems—programs like one on getting traditional Native foods approved by the Federal CDC bureaucracy for serving to Iñupiat elders in long-term care facilities in Kotzebue serviced by a NANA management services dietician (part of the same NANA that is part owner of the Red Dog Mine).[1] *The Solutions Desk* reporting was highlighted in a *New York Times* story, "From many corners, journalism seeking solutions," for its series on improving Alaska's foster care system.[2]

Developed in partnership with national PBS Digital Studios, *Indie Alaska* develops a series of videos capturing the diverse and colorful lifestyles of everyday Alaskans at work and at play, rather than the hillbilly personas portrayed in so much of today's reality TV. The program highlights the positive achievements, challenges, and human ingenuity of people living in the North who are responsible environmental stewards on the frontlines of energy, natural resources, and climate issues every day, be they artists, scholars, scientists, oil and gas engineers, or just average people with pervasive positive attitudes.

Our conversation reflected on the changes in today's media like those I described earlier, with ongoing reductions in commercial news media staffs, changes in media ownership, and increasing politicization and polarization of media like Fox News, MSNBC, and talk radio. The news landscape has changed dramatically in recent years. In today's world, too many national media celebrity moguls living and working in ivory towers in the superelite supercities of New York and Washington, DC, are increasingly out of touch with people in the rest of the country and the rest of the world as they interview each other more and more as "experts" on the news of the day. "The news media by and large missed what was happening all around it, and it was the story of a lifetime," wrote *New York Times* columnist Jim Rutenberg two days after election day in 2016 in his analysis of why so many in the national media were so shocked and "failed to predict" Donald Trump's victory."[3] Unfortunately, this growing news media disconnection plays right into the increasingly sensational atmosphere of the US political system, nowhere more so than on natural resource, energy, and environmental issues. This is not a conspiracy but an unfortunate alliance against common sense and facts.

A case study in this alliance was a 2015 *Los Angeles Times* "exposé" that cast ExxonMobil as a "climate change denier" based on a shaky premise.[4] Beginning by referring to a 25-year-old quote from a dissident shareholder, who had petitioned the board of Exxon to develop a plan to reduce carbon dioxide emissions from its production plants and facilities, the article went on to frame the company's board as somehow concealing something, simply because the company was adapting its operations to the actual warming of the Arctic, although the data was incomplete on what was actually *causing* it. According to the story, "The board's response: Exxon had studied the science of global warming and concluded it was too murky to warrant action when they said that the company's 'examination of the issue supports the conclusions that the facts today and the projection of future effects are very unclear.'" The *Times* conspiracy story then went on to imply that, at the same time, "researchers and engineers at Exxon and Imperial Oil were quietly incorporating climate change projections into the company's planning and closely studying how to adapt the company's Arctic operations to a warming planet."

What the *Times* missed was that just because Exxon did not declare what was the *cause* of global warming, there was nothing nefarious about Exxon's scientists and engineers meticulously planning their business operations to deal with the impacts of it. This is a case study in gotcha journalism at its worst.

The approach of adapting business operations to the reality of climate change while acknowledging that there is legitimate scientific debate on what is causing it in the first place is not limited to just Big Oil companies like ExxonMobil. Early in the winter of 2016, the general manager of one of North America's leading heli-ski companies said that he had just returned from a snow summit conference where leading experts from around the world gave briefings on their forecast models for snow—the commodity most important to these businesses. The expert models were predicting a continuation of the long-term winter warming trend, which had huge implications for these businesses. He said, "Regardless of what you believe the causes of global warming are, to survive moving forward, those of us in the winter sports and recreation industries must adapt our operational sides to incorporate the impacts of these changes."

And those changes may not lead to the complete Armageddon that so much of the traditional media coverage on climate change leads many of us to believe. In 2016, just 18 months after the publication of the *Los Angeles Times* exposé, another media story indicated that ExxonMobil may have been doing the right thing to ask tough questions and not follow the "politically correct" climate change herd off the cliff. At that time, the *Alaska Dispatch News* reported that leading US Geological Survey scientists completed a study that found "Melting Alaska may not accelerate climate change as expected."[5] In fact, the impartial research report, which was the first Alaska-wide inventory of naturally occurring carbon emissions, surprised many with its conclusion: "Alaska is not likely to emit as much carbon this century as they'd previously expected." As the story reported, this multiagency US government study found that "the results could reassure many who worry that the impacts of already-occurring climate change in Alaska could compromise efforts to curb greenhouse gas emissions." Traditional thinking had been that climate change in the Arctic creates a cycle of more and faster climate change, but this may not be the case, "at least through the year 2100." The US Geological Survey computer models actually found *more* vegetation growth in Alaska's Arctic than even the scientists doing the study themselves expected. That unexpected plant growth meant the vast plant life across the Arctic is actually eating huge amounts of carbon as it grows. Combining new research methods that drew on more exact estimates for thawing permafrost and the amount of carbon exposed led to a real breakthrough study, never reported on by any of the four *Los Angeles Times* writers who did the ExxonMobil climate change piece.

In fact, during all of the media-incited us-versus-them rhetoric on climate change over the past 25 years, a few companies like ExxonMobil didn't throw up their hands and say, "Let the poor people, politicians, media, and those with different ideologies freeze in the dark," as the company kept focusing some of the best technical minds on the planet on looking at ways to develop abundant Arctic energy resources to supply the world's growing energy needs in an environmentally responsible way, using the best modern science and technology. In fact, Exxon Mobil innovated; took business, technical, public relations, and political risks; engaged their scientists with others for more than 30 years, including participation in the UN Intergovernmental Panel on Climate Change since its inception; and forged ahead with a glass-half-full approach. The *Los Angeles Times* missed this more nuanced, science-based approach to the legitimate debate on the causes, as well as the impacts, of climate change, but, fortunately, other media gave us insight into it.

ExxonMobil was undertaking detailed analysis on how to adapt its oil and gas drilling operations in Canada's Arctic to the reality of warmer winters, which undisputedly do lead to shorter windows to use ice roads for transporting the drilling and related support equipment to remote Arctic energy projects, as well as longer shipping seasons for moving equipment by barge through icy northern shipping routes. Yet that has absolutely nothing to do with what is causing climate change in the first place. When a story like the *Los Angeles Times* piece reinforces popular misconceptions by misstating and manipulating facts about a complicated and important issue, it creates a ripple effect that muddies the waters for important collective consideration of natural resource issues and makes it harder for scientists and experts from all sides to bring their complicated data to a common table and collaborate. This conflict further divides important sectors of government and business, rather than bringing them to the same table to work together on real science-based solutions.

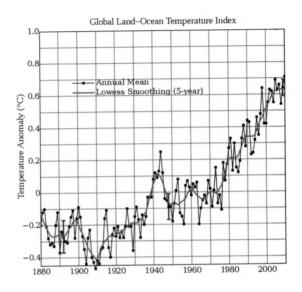

Source: *AntarcticGlaciers.org, "Climate Change."*[6]

Global temperatures have been increasing for more than 150 years since the last "little ice age." There are differing opinions on the data and underlying causes of this change, including the role of human activity and carbon emissions. A broader consideration of media coverage on the issue reveals that those in the media who have jumped on the bandwagon scapegoating those who challenge currently popular bumper-sticker rhetoric and ideas have simply furthered fears of scarcity and calamity, unnecessarily. This coverage incites emotions among readers and viewers and increases the ratings of media who push the extremes. Yet collaborative, data-driven science is increasingly finding that reality is not entirely consistent with what that worst-case zealous media coverage would have led us all to believe not so long ago.

When influential news media relapse into the sort of advocacy journalism exemplified by the *Los Angeles Times*—be it Fox News, MSNBC, or any other major media—we all need to push back and ask them those tough questions, especially when the inconvenient truth may be that they are simply inciting the societal herd to stampede toward bumper-sticker concepts as approaches to complicated natural resources issues—and potentially taking all of us off some very expensive cliffs in the process. As we ask the media tough questions and push them to go deeper in their coverage, we need to insist that the media cover good news, great achievements on environmental and economic breakthroughs, and improvements in quality of life and the environment with the same zest and fervor as when they put big businesses into the "climate change denier" box out of convenience. We need more media in the future to cover the world from a view of abundance when facts warrant it, covering glasses that are half full like the *Indie Alaska* approach, not just those that are half empty. This should be done without the scapegoating, finger-pointing and labeling of the us-versus-them approach so prevalent in far too much of today's media. We should aim for the opposite of the exposé approach used by *Los Angeles Times*, Fox News, and MSNBC.

TED Talks are a new phenomenon. Their exploding popularity shows that there is a huge market of inquisitive and critically thinking people around the globe who want to learn more about important transformational issues directly from experts. Viewed in-person and online, TED Talks are preferred by people who want more than the obsolete major TV news networks that dedicate their prime-time hours to celebrity newscasters interviewing each other about their opinions of each other.

In one particular TED Talk, "3 Ways to Fix a Broken News Industry," former ABC, Bloomberg, and *International Herald Tribune* correspondent Lara Setrakian addressed the pitfalls of media using fear to increase ratings.[7] A self-titled "industrious optimist," Setrakian says the world needs news media whose reporters have "deep domain knowledge" of the issues they are reporting on, rather than reporters who are generalists, and those "journalists should live up to their own ideals" in a world where we all should "embrace complexity in order to make sense of the world." That deeper knowledge in reporting of complex issues is something her Deep News organization is working to address through in-depth coverage of specific global issues.

In fact, an emerging positive approach to making media relevant in today's world isn't limited just to public broadcasting or faraway places like Northern Alaska. A quiet but powerful movement toward positive news media coverage is gaining momentum. *The Optimist Daily* has taken this approach globally since it started in Holland in 1995 as an independent media source committed to "solutions journalism"—the search for solutions to the challenges humanity and the planet face and intelligent optimism. *The Optimist Daily's* approach is gaining traction in some very surprising places, including with old-school media like *Newsweek*, who said *The Optimist* is the best antidote to media nastiness "you're not reading but should be," and the *San Francisco Chronicle*, who praised *The Optimist's* positive take on everything.

The Optimist Daily covers current, often divisive issues, including energy, the environment, natural resources, and human consumption, from a thoughtful and optimistic perspective. Its coverage goes beyond bumper-sticker quotes from the usual sources and "experts." In an issue that included an interview with Deepak Chopra on leadership, *The Optimist* explored how "sustainability used to be about doing less, [and] why the new sustainability is about doing more: more innovation, more good ideas."[8] Rather than just guilting readers into scarcity mindsets about all of the energy, metals, and other natural resources that we all use in everyday life and the impending destruction of civilization as we know it, *The Optimist* regularly does thoughtful pieces on things like "politically incorrect solutions to climate change," an unconventional, positive article that focused on what people in poor, developing countries are doing to innovate and adapt, rather than be indentured into further poverty by restrictions on economic development and growth imposed by do-gooders, politicians, bureaucrats, and regulators in far-away places like Brussels and Washington, DC.[9] This article explored how economic growth is necessary for the poorest people on the planet to afford the everyday necessities and more energy-efficient lifestyles readily available in developed countries around the world. They cover pieces on how in "solv[ing] our societal and environmental problems, we mustn't slow economic growth, but rather speed it up."[10] And *The Optimist* reported on why, despite popular media accounts to the contrary, "Africa is experiencing spectacular growth. More people than ever are rising above the poverty line"—and why that is actually good for the planet and environment.[11]

As another example, Alaska Public Media's *Solutions Desk* is focused on reporting what is going well in the world, in contrast to the media covering what is going wrong in the world.

In the future, if media like *The Optimist* and public broadcasting like *The Solutions Desk* can attract rave reviews from traditional media like *Newsweek* and the *San Francisco Chronicle*, this positive approach can become contagious and spread to other media. When it does, old-school media like *The New York Times* will empower their reporters to do even more work like their lengthy 2009 report "New Jungles Prompt a Debate on Rain Forests."[12] They could and should do more detailed series examining how and why economies in many third- and fourth-world countries are developing and allowing people to move up Maslow's hierarchy of needs, such as in places like rural Guatemala, where people are migrating from slash-and-burn farming in the rainforest to pursue more opportunity in urban areas as their economy grows, leading to rainforest and jungle regeneration as rural farms are abandoned.

If *Newsweek*, the *San Francisco Chronicle*, and *The New York Times* do more stories on things that are going *right* on our planet, *Los Angeles Times* editors will be forced to follow suit and dedicate four reporters at a time to stories on positive things happening on the environmental, energy, and natural resources fronts and so on and so on. I am not suggesting that the media themselves deny or sweep under the rug our environmental and energy challenges but, instead, that they take stories like a *National Geographic* exposé with stunning pictures of air and water pollution caused by China's rare earth industrial complex in Baotou and go deeper to explore real potential solutions. *National Geographic* stories on this sort of environmental challenge need to go beyond just outlining the environmental horrors of the air and water pollution around the industrial plants in China that produce 90 percent of the world's rare earth metals. They should also explore in detail real opportunities and *solutions* for the production of the rare earth metals that the increasingly technology-driven and energy-efficient world of the future needs.

Media outlets have the opportunity to become the connector that helps all of us understand the big picture of where the stuff for our stuff comes from and the role that strong economies can play as catalysts for breakthroughs in human ingenuity and technology, as well as for maintaining and strengthening community and social fibers in areas as diverse as arts and culture. Media covering these issues in the future must take this to the next level, not just reporting on earnings per share and sales but also helping connect the dots on how and why a "stable economy keeps [the] arts thriving."[13] International business publications like *The Wall Street Journal, Financial Times*, and *Business Week* should help us all understand this reality more clearly from a global perspective, as Jeffrey Hayzlett's C-Suite Radio does.

C-Suite Radio explores the challenges, successes, and failures of guests who are successful entrepreneurs, thought leaders, and innovators sharing their journeys in business and firsthand lessons relevant to their own businesses' success and growth, just as the Associated Press did in their 2011 story "Norway's oil finds shield it from economic gloom."[14] That story, rather than a typical "Major oil find in Norway will lead to increasing pollution, global warming, coastal flooding, devastation, global poverty, and the downfall of Western civilization" angle, showed readers how environmentally responsible natural resource development can be the economic foundation for a progressive country like Norway. In the United States, there is hope as well for more balanced media coverage when traditional media show signs of understanding the underlying issues behind where the stuff for our stuff comes from, particularly with regard to the energy we need to power our iGadgets, computers, and electric cars. The media should depart from the societal popularity contest approach to energy, resources, and environmental questions and go beyond clipping and pasting the same old us-versus-them quotes from "expert" sources into story templates that point toward overly simplistic solutions for complicated issues.

In order to be relevant in this new era, old-school traditional media must adapt. In the process, the media can be a connector that helps us all understand these issues more deeply, including seeing that when some say the sky is falling, the reality is that the sun may be rising on a new era of human ingenuity, breakthrough, prosperity, and improvement in human health and global environmental stewardship.

15

Better Political Leaders

Part of Hillary Clinton's bumper-sticker rhetoric during the 2016 presidential election campaign was this statement: "We are going to put a lot of coal miners and coal companies out of work."

This was in sharp contrast to her own husband's words just three months earlier in a college commencement speech that Hillary and I both attended. In that speech, the former president said, "There are so many people who feel that they're losing out in the modern world, because people either don't see, don't know, or they see them only as members of groups that they feel threatened by." He went on to explain that this wasn't about one side versus the other side. The young people pushing for immigration reform, clinging to DACA (Deferred Action for Childhood Arrivals law) and DAPA (Deferred Action for Parents of Americans and Lawful Permanent Residents law), hope to make their way in a country where their future is uncertain, and so do the coal miners, who President Clinton said think "those of us fighting climate change don't give a rip about what happens to them."[1]

Why, then, did presidential candidate Hillary Clinton seem to publicly revel in threatening those coal miners' futures?

Former president Bill Clinton's commencement address at my daughter's college graduation from Loyola-Marymount University in Los Angeles that same year included a formal introduction highlighting the unprecedented national job creation that occurred during his eight-year term, the enactment of the North American Free Trade Agreement (NAFTA), and significant environmental initiatives. A controversial figure of epic proportions, President Clinton's achievements cited in his introduction and speech that day were all based on the premise of creating a bigger pie through strong economic growth so that America could afford greater environmental stewardship, a stronger educational system, and healthcare for everyone.

Bill Clinton's vision to grow the economy so that we can better take care of the less fortunate was why my former college lecturer and early career mentor, Art Laffer—the "father of supply-side economics" and economic policy advisor to President Reagan—said he voted for Clinton for president in 1992. Laffer had shaken up my own highly partisan youthful political thinking when I was a student in a 1985 lecture. He told us that John F. Kennedy (*a Democrat!*) was one of the early true supply-side policy leaders. Laffer described Kennedy as a president who believed that lower taxes could spur more economic activity, thus creating more net government tax revenue from the ensuing increases in economic growth. What Laffer described sounded more like what I thought was a "free market" Republican approach, but it was, in fact, often espoused by Clinton during his campaign and ensuing presidency, reminding me of something my first boss at Exxon told me in 1988: "Anyone who thinks there is a difference between Democrats and Republicans doesn't understand politics."

In fact, the 1992 presidential election race between Clinton and Bush Sr. marked the end of an era in which politicians—particularly presidential candidates—tried to position themselves toward the middle ground, appealing to as many voters as possible. If voters' political views are charted on a bell curve, Clinton and Bush were both running at the middle.

For his part, Bush ran as a "compassionate conservative," based on his record of compromise and work with congressional Democrats that included a deal to increase taxes to balance the federal budget in 1990. Clinton ran as a "conservative" Democrat—one who understood the importance of creating a political and business environment that would foster the creation of more quality jobs in a growing economy that would also generate more funding for social programs, education, and environmental protection. Ultimately, during Clinton's eight years in office, he often packaged himself toward the middle of the political curve.

His legacy included one of the biggest economic booms in the world's history and the controversial NAFTA, which was hailed in that formal introduction for his Loyola commencement speech. NAFTA has since become a politically dirty word among many in the media and is often blamed by environmental groups, labor union leaders, and politicians as the cause of many of the nation's environmental and economic ills. Yet former president Clinton is still proud enough of the economic and social progress that he believes NAFTA helped unleash that he continues to include it in his personal introduction for major speeches as the centrist that he packaged himself to be in that 1992 election. Art Laffer has even said Clinton's economic policies made him "more Reagan than Reagan."[2]

That same centrist approach now sees Clinton doing things like making public appearances with the CEO of one of the world's largest mining companies as a part of the partnership I described earlier between UNICEF and the Clinton Foundation to use zinc that Teck produces from its mines to fight childhood diarrhea in some of the poorest countries in the world. Today, instead of scapegoating mining companies to pursue easy headlines, former president Clinton welcomes them inclusively to the table of people and organizations pursuing real solutions to our most pressing environmental and human health problems. Of these problems, few are more pressing than improving drinking water quality and availability to halt the plague of deaths from water-borne diarrhea–related diseases in poor countries across the globe.

Unfortunately, while Bill Clinton was welcoming leaders in the global mining industry to sit at the same table and talk about real solutions, Hillary Clinton was publicly trying to incite the herd to stampede by vilifying the miners. As *The Washington Post* reported during the 2016 presidential campaign, she was facing pressure from the herd, because "Democrats, in general, have become much more willing to embrace liberal policies over the past couple of decades."[3]

An inclusive approach is needed now more than ever from our political leaders. Al Gore followed this approach during the eight years he served as Clinton's vice president, when Gore was involved in numerous pro-business initiatives, including the complicated multinational production-sharing agreements that got ExxonMobil and Shell into the deals with Russian oil companies and the Russian government itself to pursue those major offshore energy projects on Sakhalin Island that I discussed earlier. Yet we never heard about those oil and gas deals in Gore's 2000 presidential election campaign against Texas governor George Bush Jr. Gore, who was described by *The Economist* in 1999 as a "centrist," moved away from the political center in that campaign and toward the herd on the far left. At the same time, Bush, who had earned high marks among nontraditional Republican constituencies in the education and Latino communities as a moderate governor in Texas, with a proven track record of bipartisanship and working across the aisle, started running away from the middle and toward the far right.

That year's election marked the unfortunate dawn of a new political era, as Bush Jr. and Gore ran as far away from each other as they could. In doing so, they ran away from the center, where most voters reside, and focused their campaigns on chasing voters at the respective extreme ends of the spectrum. This new tactic was designed by their respective political operatives to get those extreme voters out to the polls, which fit the agendas of media and interest groups pursuing those same extremes. The convergence was also perfectly suited to the new 24-hour news cycles adopted by the likes of Fox News, MSNBC, and CNN. The networks' own media extremism is designed to maximize controversy and appeal to certain core demographic groups, thus increasing advertising sales to companies targeting consumers in those groups.

Bush's presidency was then marked not by that bipartisanship and work across the aisle that had made him so popular as governor of Texas but, instead, by agendas of political operatives. In the process, those operatives also chased away more thoughtful mainstream cabinet members and advisors, like secretary of state Colin Powell. At the same time, Gore furthered his move into the extreme left as he pursued his new brand as environmental zealot out to save the world from the perceived impending destruction by oil companies and energy developments—like those he previously helped support in Russia.

We need to turn this around. We need to change who is leading and who is following and move to a place where political leaders lead by modeling cooperation, working together, and solving problems rather than creating them. This sort of cooperation was a hallmark of the final two years of Ronald Reagan's presidency. The book *The Kennedy Half-Century* said, "In an age of punishing political polarization, when the right and the left are constantly at each other's throats, President Kennedy—a forceful partisan in his time—has become a standard exemplar of bipartisanship."[4] Now more than ever, we need the sort of cooperation exhibited when then–Vice President Al Gore worked closely with his Russian counterpart, Viktor Chernomyrdin, in the bilateral commission they formed to further economic cooperation between the two countries. We need a world where leaders work across the aisle for the common good, instead of against each other for their own reelection. I have seen this bipartisanship firsthand on controversial legislative initiatives around autism insurance coverage, youth tobacco, childhood obesity prevention, teen suicide prevention, numerous other public health initiatives, and environmentally sound natural resource development. If more politicians will step across the aisle to work together on initiatives like these, their success will breed more success.

We need a world where political leaders are accountable for problem-solving, not just generating the slickest and most memorable bumper-sticker slogans. To get there, we must move away from politicians whose primary objective is increasing contributions from special interests and super PACs—be those affiliated with Tea Party activists, labor unions, or environmental groups. A senior executive from one of the world's largest mining companies told me after Harry Reid became US Senate majority leader and Barrack Obama was elected president that he had worked with both when they were in the US Senate and had found each understood the importance and value of environmentally responsible mining in creating jobs and producing the metals and materials we need in everyday life. His experience was that Obama, as a senator from Illinois, a manufacturing state where Caterpillar is headquartered and which supplies the equipment used in mining and related industries, and Reid, as a senator from Nevada, which is America's largest gold-producing state, were both pro-mining because they understood that we could have both quality jobs in mining and strong environmental protection. Yet when Reid became US Senate majority leader and Obama became president, both dramatically changed course and publicly joined the herd pushing more extreme environmental agendas that were more politically correct when the spotlight was on them. This is part of the trend where politicians like Al Gore and Sarah Palin abandon those of us in the middle to chase the extremes.

In the future, if more of us take the time to understand where the stuff for our stuff comes from, more of us will insist that political leaders from both parties be thoughtful and brave enough not to join the politically correct herds. Those who define themselves through bumper-sticker *Save the planet* and *Drill, baby, drill* rhetoric for the sake of political convenience to get elected need to be shifted to a more thoughtful environment, which starts with each of us, from the bottom up. And there are signs of hope for that shift, despite the political extremism we see so often in the consideration of natural resources issues in the political world.

A new way

US senators Ron Wyden, a Democrat from Oregon, and Lisa Murkowski, a Republican from Alaska, drew strong praise during their time serving together as the ranking members of the US Senate Committee on Energy and Natural Resources. In 2012, in a public display of bipartisanship that was part of agreements they forged over several years on numerous complicated energy and environmental issues, Murkowski said, "My friend, I extend my hand, because we're going to work together. . . . We're going to set the tone; we're going to set the standard." During a joint interview at a breakfast hosted by Congressional Quarterly Roll Call, Murkowski said, "We both recognize there's a lot of pent-up demand out there." As *Politico* reported at the time, "Across town, committee member Senator Joe Manchin expressed hope that the panel's new reigning duo will shake up five years of frozen national energy policy." "I have never been more optimistic than I am right now with Ron Wyden and Lisa Murkowski," Manchin said. Prior to the Murkowski/Wyden initiative, Congress had not passed major energy legislation for years.[5]

An endangered species in Washington today, Murkowski and Wyden worked together across the aisle for several years to build consensus on environment, energy, and natural resource issues.

Murkowski later told a small group of us gathered at a coffee shop in an Alaskan ski town that she and Wyden had agreed on nearly 80 percent of the issues and had focused on making things happen rather than getting stuck on areas of disagreement. This was a tough task on a senate committee that included extremists like Bernie Sanders and Al Franken. Yet it was an approach reminiscent of some of Murkowski and Wyden's predecessors from both parties, back in the days when Alaska Republican Ted Stevens worked cooperatively with Democratic Louisiana senator Bennett Johnston on numerous energy and natural resource issues. Those bipartisan efforts also included Republican Stevens's work with Washington State Democrats Henry Jackson and Warren Magnuson on fisheries conservation issues, which included passage of legislation that set the long-term regulatory framework for critical science-based conservation and management of our nation's offshore fisheries resources.

Senators Murkowski and Wyden, while members of different political parties, distinguished themselves in the US Senate by sticking to their core principles while working together to forge consensus on the art of the possible. This meant they didn't always agree yet got things done and worked to avoid the us-versus-them partisan headline grabbing that has become so prevalent in Washington. Today, we need bipartisan consensus more than ever.

16

A Better Future

Right out of the world of the old *Jetsons* cartoon, news media in 2017 started talking more and more about new space-age technologies for transporting people and goods. Uber and Google made headlines with their work on flying cars, while on a bigger scale Lockheed Martin and others already in the aviation world, as well as Amazon and Walmart, worked on morphing an old-school flying technology into a modern, state-of-the-art aircraft that could move large numbers of people and products using a fraction of the energy of conventional airplanes. These breakthrough innovations which could significantly reduce the human footprint for transportation were not being developed by a government subsidy or mandate or self-branded eco-friendly company with bright green labels.

In Lockheed Martin's case, they were one of the world's oldest and largest defense contractors developing new aircraft called *hybrid* airships, which have the potential to move people, freight, energy, minerals, medical supplies, and food across vast distances with a smaller and a far more energy-efficient footprint than traditional aircraft or trucks—a true potential breakthrough in how freight could be delivered to consumers far more affordably and efficiently. This technology could also facilitate the development of new mines to supply the world's growing tech and high-energy-efficiency economy with the metals necessary to support them.

Out in the middle of the California desert, I have had the opportunity to visit the top-secret facility where Lockheed Martin's Skunk Works team has invented countless aviation breakthroughs over the past 70 years, from the famous stealth fighter to old-fashioned passenger airplanes, helicopters, rockets, smart missiles, the U-2 spy plane, and now the hybrid airship known as the LMH-1.

The author in front of the California test facility

Lockheed Martin's new LMH-1 is the latest aviation breakthrough. The culmination of over 20 years of work, the LMH-1 is a hybrid airship capable of carrying 20 tons of payload and up to 19 passengers over ranges up to 1400 nautical miles. It's able to circle the globe on a single tank of gas. This is not an old-fashioned blimp;

this new generation of airship has the potential to dramatically lower cargo transportation costs to remote areas, which today often require construction of expensive new roads or highly expensive air transport.

As one aviation executive said, "The airship offers an environmentally friendly solution to the problem of cargo transport in [places like] the Brazilian rainforest."[1]

These sorts of aviation breakthroughs being explored by the likes of Lockheed Martin, Uber, and Google, along with the flying drones to deliver individual packages being pursued by Amazon and UPS, may reduce the human footprint from the jungles of South America and Africa to the Arctic, improving the economies of local communities and villages around the globe while decreasing the human footprint of road construction everywhere from growing urban supercities to remote villages in jungles and the Arctic. For communities in remote jungles and parts of the Arctic with some of the highest costs of living on the planet due to their remote nature, airships alone could greatly lower shipping costs by using aircraft that's less expensive and more fuel-efficient than today's old-fashioned airplanes.

In pursuing these disruptive technologies, companies are doing just the opposite of what former Eastman Kodak chief marketing officer and leading business media voice Jeffrey Hayzlett describes as the downfall of old-school household name Kodak. Hayzlett said in a presentation in 2016 that "Kodak didn't go bankrupt when they filed Chapter 11 bankruptcy in 2012, but back in 1975." At that time, he said, an inventor inside Kodak put together a metal box camera device and took a picture of his own pet dog—without using film. Showing what may have been the first digital camera to Kodak decision-makers back then, Hayzlett said, the inventor was uniformly dismissed by senior executives and managers, because "Kodak sells film." Selling that film was the foundation of how the company made billions of dollars each year, and it had made Kodak a huge part of the fabric of American life. Their pictures, distributed in their famous yellow envelopes, sat in virtually every home and office across the country for a generation.

Yet Kodak's cornerstone film business has since gone the way of the black-and-white TV, eight-track player, payphone, and floppy disk. As Hayzlett says in his book *Think Big, Act Bigger*, successful companies are led by those who don't rest on their laurels but, instead, take risks and think out of their traditional boxes.[2] They focus on where they're going rather than on where they've been.

In the future, companies who make game-changing break-throughs and advancements for society will be the ones who will thrive, especially in the transportation, energy, and natural resources fields, where leading-edge technology is core to what they do and what they will accomplish in the future.

A case study in remaining relevant as human technologies advance, Lockheed's Skunk Works team has invented dozens of aviation breakthroughs since World War II, and their corporate management to this day keeps the Skunk Works team separate from the rest of the company, lest their thinking and ingenuity be contaminated by the company's own corporate bureaucracy. The advancements in moving people and cargo that companies like these are pursuing have potentially transformational economic and environmental benefits for mankind and the environment. These sorts of technology changes have the potential to advance environmental stewardship in a world with a growing population, and an increasing number of innovative corporations will be the catalysts for countless other breakthroughs in human innovation and technology as they integrate new ideas and out-of-the-box thinking into their daily activity as it relates to energy efficiency, environmental stewardship, and the broader human footprint.

On the individual human communications front, new innovators will bridge the digital divide between high-speed fiber-connected supercities and unconnected poorer parts of the world that lack even basic telecommunications, much less the economic and social benefits of high-speed Internet for education, healthcare, and human connection. Companies like OneWeb are developing inexpensive, small-scale plates in lieu of satellite dishes for homes in poor and remote parts of the globe to connect them to the Internet via a new network of satellites on a north–south orbit rather than the traditional east–west orbit around the equator. OneWeb's vision is so compelling that they have attracted hundreds of millions of dollars in investment from the likes of Virgin Group founder Richard Branson and Airbus.

All of this demonstrates the incredible potential for human good through combining technology with the smart use of mineral and energy resources. Moving into the future, what can we, as individuals, and other corporations learn from this? First and foremost, the most successful entrepreneurs and companies will be those who are most adept at paving the way for improvements in global environmental stewardship. They will be the ones who spearhead the deployment of new ideas and inventions from some surprising sources—going the way of Lockheed Martin, Amazon, and Tesla rather than Kodak. It will be innovative corporations who implement breakthroughs that decrease the relative human footprint on the planet in the face of growing populations, for the good of the planet and mankind. Along the way, these companies will find ever more innovative ways to improve our collective environmental stewardship, not just in obvious areas like water quality, sewage treatment, and air quality, but in other areas we haven't even thought of yet in the production, manufacturing, and distribution process.

Mining companies like Teck, whose Red Dog mine cleaned up naturally acidic Red Dog Creek, which I discussed earlier in this book, while also providing jobs, opportunities, and funding for the Northwest Arctic local education system, partnering with global charities like UNICEF and world leaders like former president Bill Clinton in initiatives like the one I also described earlier for childhood diarrhea prevention, can expand these beneficial initiatives even further. They can potentially save the lives of millions of the world's poorest children in India, South America, and Africa. Underlying all this, mining companies are already quietly driving significant change in how they produce the minerals we need for far more than just vitamins and smartphones. In places where the processes that turn raw ore into those final metals are water-intensive, one of the world's largest mining companies, Anglo American, is investing in processes intended to make many of their mines water neutral by 2030.

Education can also improve when companies investing in truly sustainable manufacturing processes and technologies partner with educational institutions like the sustainable manufacturing program at the California State University, Chico.[3] This program's partners are as diverse as one of the world's largest medical device manufacturers, NASA, and the Sierra Nevada Brewing Company. Sustainable manufacturing is an emerging integrated field of study that combines technical feasibility with environmental responsibility and economic viability in assessing the entire manufacturing process—from start to finish.

As graduates from programs like these enter the workforce, it will be the best, most adept companies who hire them and thus transfer the benefits of these approaches to us all. Companies who employ these approaches and take advantage of these breakthroughs can thrive if they can put this into practice in building more environmentally sustainable housing, transportation systems, workplaces, and healthcare facilities. These companies will be the catalysts for more environmentally smart, sustainable, and energy-efficient communities and cities around the globe—especially in rapidly urbanizing China, India, and Africa. This could mean new hospitals being built with the latest in medical, construction, and energy-efficient technologies, potentially at a fraction of the cost of expensive, old-school versions of brick-and-mortar hospitals based on 1950s design models.

These sorts of changes may be embraced and deployed not just by traditional companies like Lockheed Martin, Teck, and Anglo American but also by those relative newcomers like Uber, Amazon, Tesla, and other companies we haven't even heard of yet emerging in China, India, South America, and Africa.

Uber itself is a classic disruptive technology company that has married old-school technology (cars) with new ways of being in today's modern, evolving world. The company owns little more than a smartphone app, yet in just a few short years, Uber and its competitors like Lyft are alleviating the need for many people to even own their own cars. In the process, this new company is indirectly improving the planet by more efficiently using metals, plastics, and energy in the everyday mass production of cars, as fewer underused cars may need to be built to sit idle 20 hours per day in the first place, making for potentially huge reductions in the human footprint in the process. Old-school car manufacturers like Ford are taking note, launching campaigns directed at potential Uber drivers rather than just traditional single-family car markets.

Just as better corporations will be the catalysts for breakthroughs on the energy and natural resources, transportation, and environmental fronts, so will they be in healthcare. This will occur as biotechnology companies like Biogen and Merck or emerging new competitors we haven't heard of in places like Brazil make new breakthroughs in treatment and potential cures for various forms of cancer, hepatitis, and Alzheimer's disease. Brazil may be on track to becoming part of a new Uber of healthcare, a place where the online news site *BIOtechNOW* reported that, in 2012, already had nearly 90 biotech companies working on "the development of new medications (small molecules and biological), diagnostics, vaccines, cell therapy, regenerative medicine and tissue engineering, advanced methods for assisted reproduction, genetic and molecular testing, etc."[4] Brazil's emergence as a global biotech player is a result of the country using the wealth generated from energy and mineral development as a foundation to reinvent itself and diversify.

Just like the deployment of learning in sustainable manufacturing from schools like Chico State in the industrial sector, drug companies will increasingly partner with leading academic institutions like the University of Washington, doing breakthrough medical research and deploying those discoveries for the benefit of all of us. These breakthroughs will require the use of metals like copper, which will, in turn, be mined by companies using ever more innovative ways to produce it.

On the energy front, leading companies who continue to invest in new energy technologies and also partner with leading-edge academic institutions, like ExxonMobil's partnership with Stanford's Global Climate and Energy Project, will spearhead and deploy new technologies that could lead to ever more efficient and less pollutive energy production and use. The energy companies of the future who embrace this path will thrive. Old-school transportation companies like the Union Pacific Railroad, who are already deploying leading-edge technology into their transportation businesses along with new, ultra-energy-efficient locomotives to move the materials we all need, have the potential to literally be trains on the tracks to the future.

As all of this unfolds, creative people will be the catalysts and better corporations will be the energy for these changes, and standards of living around the globe will increase more dramatically than ever before in the process. The companies who are at the leading edge of this wave will thrive. Those who rest on their laurels and follow societal bumper-sticker approaches will be left behind like Kodak's film. To make this happen, we as a society need to push corporate leaders to be less risk averse in pursuing new opportunities. We need to move society away from the us-versus-them mentality so prevalent today that vilifies corporations as evil, faceless entities so that we can all work together. In the process, we can support those companies making meaningful changes rather than those using manipulative slogans, with our minds, wallets, and investment dollars.

The art of the possible

Although increasingly bumper-sticker political and media rhetoric too often dominate the approach to answering our most important energy, natural resource, and environmental questions, there is another path forward. Even with politicians, media, government regulators, and interest groups all taking advantage of the growing discord and disconnect to further their own agendas, I see something very different on the horizon.

Indeed, the world is at an economic crossroads, and if we look back at the past 50-plus years, there is reason for hope—nowhere more so than on the environmental and natural resource fronts. Following

World War II, Europe and Japan were literally torn to pieces. Their environments, physical infrastructure, economic foundation, and psychological states had been shattered. They were in much the same situation as South Africa at the end of the Apartheid era and Eastern Europe after the fall of the Berlin Wall. Their challenges were similar to what many of the world's most struggling countries face today. Yet a look back at the post–World War II European, post-Apartheid South African, and post–Cold War Eastern European experiences reveals examples of incredible progress, despite daunting circumstances. These are places where the forces of political, government, business, community, and cultural change converged and worked together for the common good. And it can be that way again in the quest for intelligent, sustainable development.

As the book *The European Economy since 1945* describes, the lives of most Europeans have been transformed almost beyond recognition since World War II ended.[5] As recently as 1950, many of Europe's residents heated their homes with coal, cooled their food with ice, and lacked indoor plumbing. Yet "today, their lives are eased and enriched by natural-gas furnaces, electric refrigerators, and an array of electronic gadgets that boggles the mind. Gross domestic product per capita, what the income of a typical resident of Europe will buy, tripled in the second half of the twentieth century." The book graphically describes how, as all of this has unfolded, the European quality of life improved as the average "hours worked declined by one-third, providing an enormous increase in leisure time. Life expectancy lengthened as a result of improved nutrition and advances in medical science." Indeed, history reveals that most "Europeans today [are] enormously better off than their grandparents were fifty years ago." As the European Bank for Reconstruction and Development found in 2016, the happiness gap between Eastern and Western Europe disappeared just 25 years after the fall of the Berlin Wall.[6] And there is no reason why this success cannot be applied to the most challenging global questions we face today.

When it comes to the critical need for energy and mineral production and use, the logjams must be broken. That starts with fostering innovation and then applying it to projects that produce the energy and minerals we all need, the facilities that refine them, and consumers who use them in today's world. In fact, one of the most transformational global economic, environmental, and natural resource changes in the history of mankind is right on the horizon —in China of all places. This transformation is now at a fork in the road between the old Chinese approach of a scorched environment, similar to that of Russia and Eastern Europe in the communist era, and the use of modern environmental technology to transform an entire society toward quantum improvements in environmental stewardship. In choosing its path, China won't wait seven to eight years for our forces of *Drill, baby, drill* and *Save the planet* to tell them which turn to take.

China has a growing middle class, estimated at 150 to 200 million people and growing. Several hundred million more Chinese are on a path to rise into the middle class in the next two decades, with global forecasting experts at Ernst and Young projecting that "by 2030, around one billion people in China could be middle class—as much as 70 percent of its projected population."[7]

In just half of most of our lifetimes, China has gone from one of the poorest countries in the world to one of the most prosperous. It is now a country with a middle-class population two-thirds the size of the entire United States—and still growing.

That development and consumption could lead to even more of the sort of negative environmental impacts cited by so many, including myself earlier in this book. Most of the next generation of Chinese citizens will live in modern, middle-class cities, built of cement, steel, and copper. This impending transition will lead to one of the largest, fastest increases in global use of minerals and energy in the history of mankind as well, eloquently described by Gianni Kovačević in his book *My Electrician Drives a Porsche*.[8] This increasing Chinese demand for minerals and energy dominates so much of the discourse on both business and the environment.

Yet I see this as a catalyst for unprecedented opportunity in science- and technology-based responsible environmental stewardship. Most of these people will be moving from poor, agricultural settings, with associated water and air pollution, into modern, more energy- and resource-efficient cities. As these people move into state-of-the-art modern cities, Chinese leaders have the opportunity to take advantage of the latest technology breakthroughs in areas like energy-efficient housing and power generation and, in fact, are already starting to do so with decisions like converting Beijing's fleet of nearly 70,000 old-school, gasoline-burning taxi cabs to all-electric models. These electric taxis are still made of mineral and oil products, but they rely on far more efficient energy sources to power them. As this unfolds, it is ironic that the same China I have chastised so many times in this book for low and nonexistent environmental standards may be on the cusp of raising the environmental bar in many ways, while the United States remains increasingly stalled in us-versus-them paralysis.

The Chinese are also increasingly moving forward with intelligent development of energy-efficient housing and modern rail systems without waiting eight to ten years to complete their permitting and decision-making processes. They're not waiting for a societal popularity contest to tell them what to do. They are getting their environmental house in order by improving how they develop and potentially leapfrogging us. Think of it: cities with ultramodern transportation systems, high-speed trains, power plants with state-of-the-art energy efficiency and pollution-control technology, including cleaner burning coal, oil, and natural gas; wind and solar to power those cities; and likely technologies we haven't even thought of yet. Modern Chinese cities may look more like a scene out of *The Jetsons* than the American rustbelt. In the process, old smog-filled cities like Beijing have the opportunity to transition to cleaner air, a foundational change for cities like London and Los Angeles. As this wave continues, an underlying question is *Who will supply China with the energy, materials, technology, and innovations for this transition?*

In fact, even with this staggering growth in China's middle class, per-person copper use in China today is actually less than the United States. This is a result of this development coming very recently and of China increasingly using the latest technology in much of what they do. China may be using copper more efficiently than many other countries that developed when copper was plentiful and cheap, using 1950s and 1960s technologies, but its continuing development will still require huge amounts of copper and metals, as well as plastics and other oil products.

If China can modernize using the latest, most efficient technologies for natural resource development, so can the other emerging economies Wall Street has labeled the *BRIC* countries—Brazil, Russia, India, and China—because of their leading growth among emerging markets. These countries are all potentially part of a modernization trend in which smart people may find even more new ways to use old and new technologies, like hybrid airships, electric busses, LNG-powered trains, wireless transmission of electricity, and the seemingly far-fetched new inventions like flying cars that Uber and

Google are pursuing. All of this is to move people and goods with greater environmental and economic efficiency.

Yet all of this efficient use of mineral and energy resources will not eliminate the need to produce energy and minerals smartly—just the opposite. As *The Christian Science Monitor* reported in 2017, there are new companies experimenting with something called "post organic sustainable farming," which involves growing the agricultural products we need indoors, in state-of-the-art highly energy-efficient shelves that are stacked in rows that grow more productive crops using a fraction of the water, fertilizer, and pesticides of even modern outdoor farming. "More than 100 times more productive on the same footprint of land . . . [allowing] crops to grow year-round, at a faster rate, and using 95 percent less water than traditional agriculture . . . [using] LED lighting that mimics the sun, and a 24-hour monitoring to ensure a reliable yield without wasting resources."[9] This technology is already being deployed in Alaska by start-up company Vertical Harvest Hydroponics, who put it into old-school shipping containers to remote communities to grow produce locally in places facing an obesity epidemic as pre-packaged long-shelf-life potato chips and soda pop have become food staples for many. Increasing future consumer demand for these sorts of breakthrough high-tech, highly energy-efficient technologies also requires metals and plastics for the LED lights themselves, the power generated to provide electricity for those lights, and even the shelving that replaces traditional soil.

As new supercities and societies emerge around the globe in response to this increasing prosperity, they can build the latest innovations and energy-efficient smart transportation systems. New supercities worldwide have the opportunity to plan for this from the start, following in the footsteps of places like Denver, where rail lines were installed to the airport *before* the surrounding areas were built.

Modern train running into the Denver airport

Too many decision makers in the United States have been slow to learn this forethought, that we need to build infrastructure for the future—not brush it off, especially as it relates to energy-efficient public transportation and smart resource development. Instead of bickering and leaving the work for future generations, we should develop a consensus on whether our standards are either too slack or too rigorous—and, where necessary, fix them. This goes beyond just saying that we need more electric cars and energy-efficient mass transit. It means a more progressive and encompassing approach that considers where the metals for our electric cars and trains will come from, along with the energy to power them. It is time for us to come together in unity on a common strategy to advance where we are going in a more sustainable, progressive approach to human development in the future.

In the United States, we have the opportunity to lead the world into a new way of thinking about development and move past us-versus-them rhetoric while we export our pollution to other parts of the planet that are out of sight and out of mind.

As we move toward the modern age of *The Jetsons*, new approaches to transportation, like drones and hybrid airships, could move crops and produce from rural African farms to growing African cities far more efficiently and cheaply, decreasing food spoilage and waste and improving human health through greater availability of fresh fruit and vegetables for city dwellers. Breakthroughs that increase crop yields may greatly decrease the quantities of water needed to grow food and would thus decrease the long-term agricultural footprint of African agriculture—just like I saw in Guatemala, where abandonment of slash-and-burn subsistence farms is leading to regeneration of rain forest and wildlife habitats. Eventually, even these developing countries can adopt those less-soil-using, highly energy-efficient indoor farming methods I described earlier in this chapter.

All of this means we will need metals and energy more than ever. It has to come from someplace. Done right, this requires smart global environmental stewardship where production of natural resources is not held hostage under complex, confusing, and contradictory regulatory systems that slow and impede responsible development. Instead, stronger energy and environmental stewardship for the smart use of these resources and producing them to the highest environmental and technological standards also requires a more efficient, fact- and science-based process that is applied clearly and transparently.

This is a world where modernizing cities in Africa, China, and India may be built to ever-increasing standards of sustainability, energy efficiency, and environmental stewardship and include sleek housing with plentiful parks, made of minerals and powered by energy developed with modern science to the highest standard. This could move the limits of human ingenuity. Along the way, we can eliminate homelessness, sex tourism, hunger, malnutrition, and childhood diarrhea deaths and increase human health and the number of high-quality jobs. Moving toward a world where Madagascar and other African countries who lack basic necessities follow Chile in responsibly using their resource wealth to lift up entire societies, American Indians and other indigenous people around the globe can follow Alaska Natives in the Arctic regions of Northwest Alaska out of the fourth world and into the first while improving environmental stewardship in the process.

We can only see these possibilities from an optimistic glass-half-full perspective. These possibilities are endless for good, and they are within our reach, waiting to be unleashed. Let's get on with it.

Acknowledgments

My mom, Pat, who set an example by blazing many trails throughout her life, including starting her first book when she was 70 years old, and my father, Bill, whose tenacity in the face of adversity and indelible spirit set an inspirational example for how to always push forward, and my sister, Susan, who exemplifies both of their spirits. My "second father," Rick, who taught me the importance of critical thinking and questioning everything.

My daughter Tonya, who continuously engages me in policy conversations and out-of-the-box thinking and provided insight into the psychology and subtle messaging of politicians, interest groups, and businesses that are explored in this book. My daughter Megan, who did such outstanding copyediting of this book and continually reminded me to be more concise and to "drop the run-on sentences." My youngest daughter, Mia, who gives all of us inspiration.

Wendy, who urged me to get on with it and "pull the trigger and launch your darn book!"

Chris Benguhe, my outstanding editor and coach, who played an invaluable role in turning this book from rant to reality.

The many mentors I have had through the years, from traditional teachers and professors to business mentors, sponsors, and life teachers. At every turn, someone new has always come along, proving that "when the student is ready, the teacher will arrive."

Notes

CHAPTER 1

1. David Rose, "Myth of Arctic Meltdown," *Daily Mail* (August 30, 2014).

2. "Supplier Responsibility," Apple, accessed April 16, 2018, https://www.apple.com/supplier-responsibility/.

3. Paul Lester, "4 Ways to Slay Energy Vampires This Halloween," US Department of Energy website (October 29, 2015), https://energy.gov/articles/4-ways-slay-energy-vampires-halloween.

4. Bryan Walsh, "The Surprisingly Large Energy Footprint of the Digital Economy," *Time* (August 14, 2013), http://science.time.com/2013/08/14/power-drain-the-digital-cloud-is-using-more-energy-than-you-think/.

5. Robert Guy Matthews, "Permits Drag on US Mining Projects," *Wall Street Journal* (February 8, 2010), https://www.wsj.com/articles/SB10001424052748703822404575019123766644644.

CHAPTER 3

1. World Bank, "Colombia: Winning the War on Poverty and Inequality Despite the Odds," World Bank (January 14, 2016), http://www.worldbank.org/en/news/feature/2016/01/14/colombia-winning-the-war-on-poverty-and-inequality-despite-the-odds.

2. Tradingeconomics.com

3. World Bank, Poverty Reduction and Equity website.

4. Penguin, 2010.

5. Carl Wiens, "The Experts: How the U.S. Oil Boom Will Change the Markets and Geopolitics," *Wall Street Journal* (March 27, 2013), https://www.wsj.com/articles/SB10001424127887324105204578382690249436084.

CHAPTER 4

1. Marketwire, "Public Health Experts Recognized for Work in Zinc Deficiency," *Marketwired* (January 28, 2011), http://www.marketwired.com/press-release/public-health-experts-recognized-for-work-in-zinc-deficiency-1387015.htm.

2. *Zinc and Health Quarterly Newsletter* 12 (October 2014).

3. Elizabeth Bluemink, "Mine Moves Up in National Toxic Release Rankings," *Juneau Empire* (May 12, 2005), http://juneauempire.com/stories/051205/sta_20050512025.shtml#.WPUdYBLyuQM.

4. World Bank, "Madagascar: Measuring the Impact of the Political Crisis," World Bank (June 5, 2013), http://www.worldbank.org/en/news/feature/2013/06/05/madagascar-measuring-the-impact-of-the-political-crisis.

5. Ian Johnson, "In China, 'Once the Villages Are Gone, the Culture Is Gone,'" *New York Times* (February 1, 2014), https://www.nytimes.com/2014/02/02/world/asia/once-the-villages-are-gone-the-culture-is-gone.html.

CHAPTER 5

1. Salary.com.

2. David J. Miller, "Project Earth: Connecting Tomorrow's Environmental Leaders Around the World," *Adirondack Journal of Environmental Studies* 17 (2011), http://www.ajes.org/v17/miller2011.php.

3. Alaska Mental Health Trust Authority, 2014 Annual Report, http://mhtrust.org/mhtawp/wp-content/uploads/2015/01/0507_Trust -Annual-Report-2014.pdf.

4. Bjoern H. Amland and George Jahn, "Norway Oil Finds Shield It from Economic Gloom," CSN News (August 31, 2011), http://www .cnsnews.com/news/article/norways-oil-finds-shield-it-economic-gloom.

5. International Association of Oil and Gas Producers (OGP), *Strategic Health Management: Principles and Guidelines for the Oil and Gas Industry* (OGP, 2000), http://www.ogp.org.uk/pubs/307.pdf.

6. Cheryl Pellerin, "DOD, U.S. Agencies Help Afghanistan Exploit Mineral Wealth," US Department of Defense (July 30, 2012), http://archive .defense.gov/news/newsarticle.aspx?id=117330.

CHAPTER 6

1. Elisabeth Rosenthal, "New Jungles Prompt a Debate on Rain Forests," *New York Times* (January 29, 2009), http://www.nytimes.com/2009 /01/30/science/earth/30forest.html.

2. The World Bank, "Guatemala: Overview," World Bank (April 7, 2017), http://www.worldbank.org/en/country/guatemala/overview.

3. US Agency for International Development (USAID), *Guatemala: Environment Situation Analysis*, USAID website (March 6, 2017), https://www.usaid.gov/guatemala/environment.

4. USAID, *Factors Affecting Homicide Rates in Guatemala 2000-2013: A Study of the Municipalities of Guatemala, Mixco, and Villa Nueva*, USAID (February 7, 2014), http://pdf.usaid.gov/pdf_docs/PA00KDR8.pdf.

CHAPTER 7

1. Joseph Chamie and Barry Mirkin, "Russian Demographics: The Perfect Storm," Yaleglobal online (December 11, 2014), http://yaleglobal.yale .edu/content/russian-demographics-perfect-storm.

CHAPTER 8

1. Emma Young, "How Iceland Got Teens to Say No to Drugs," *The Atlantic* (January 19, 2017), https://www.theatlantic.com/health/archive/2017/01 /teens-drugs-iceland/513668.

2. Mohammed Rafiq, "Football: Iceland Shock England at Euro 2016," *Gulf News* (June 28, 2016), http://gulfnews.com/multimedia/framed /sport/football-iceland-shock-england-at-euro-2016-1.1853748.

CHAPTER 9

1. Tamar Levin, "David Helfand's New Quest," *New York Times* (January 20, 2012), http://www.nytimes.com/2012/01/22/education/edlife/david -helfands-new-quest.html?_r=0.

CHAPTER 10

1. Chris Weber, "Dirty Secrets Under the Bleachers: When Landfills Become Sports Arenas," *Mental Floss* (October 7, 2008), http://mentalfloss.com /article/19795/dirty-secrets-under-bleachers-when-landfills-become -sports-arenas.

2. US Environmental Protection Agency (EPA), *Closed Waste Sites as Community Assets: A Guide for Municipalities, Landfill Owners, and Regulators* (EPA/600/R-14/349, 2014).

3. Chambers Bay Golf Course, "Site History: From Native Land to Industrial Mining to Public Park," Chambers Bay Golf Course website (February 15,

2015), http://www.chambersbaygolf.com/2015/02
/site-history-from-native-land-to-industrial-mining-to-public-park.

4. National Petroleum Reserve in Alaska (NPRA), *The Inupiat View* (NPRA 105(c), vol. 1(b), March 1979), http://www.inupiatgov.com/wp-content /gallery/npra/TheInupiatView.pdf.

5. "EPA's Budget and Spending," United States Environmental Protection Agency, https://www.epa.gov/planandbudget/budget

CHAPTER 11

1. Patrick B. Dorsey, senior vice president, secretary, and general counsel, Tiffany & Co., letter to Elizabeth M. Murphy, Secretary, Securities and Exchange Commission, September 29, 2010.

2. Christine Hauser, "Patagonia, REI, and Other Outdoor Retailers Protest Trump's Decision to Shrink Utah Monuments," *The New York Times* (December 5, 2017), https://www.nytimes.com/2017/12/05 /business/patagonia-trump-utah.html.

   David Miller, "Stop Orvis! In Their Opposition to the Pebble Mine," SME Community (April 17, 2013), http://community.smenet.org/browse/blogs /blogviewer?BlogKey=9f0cf2e1-9572-4c58-8d8f-ae75166b9f02&ssopc=1.

CHAPTER 12

1. Gallup, "What Everyone in the World Wants: A Good Job," Gallup (June 9, 2015), http://www.gallup.com/businessjournal/183527/everyone-world -wants-good-job.aspx.

2. Lily Kuo, "Kenya's National Electrification Campaign Is Taking Less than Half the Time It Took in America," Quartz Africa (January 16, 2017), https://qz.com/882938/kenya-is-rolling-out-its-national-electricity -program-in-half-the-time-it-took-america.

3. http://www.care2.com/greenliving/author/ode1.

CHAPTER 13

1. Walter Lamar, "Cleaning Up the Environment, Starting with Reservations," *Indian Country Today* (May 4, 2013), https://indiancountrymedianetwork .com/news/opinions/cleaning-up-the-environment-starting-with -reservations.

2. Caroline Kende-Robb, "How Africa's Natural Resources Can Lift Millions out of Poverty," CNN (July 25, 2013), http://www.cnn.com /2013/07/25/opinion/africas-natural-resources-millions-poverty.

CHAPTER 14

1. Anne Hillman, "Mixing Science with Traditional Knowledge, Researchers Hope to Get Seal Oil on the Menu," Alaska Public Media (March 5, 2018), https://www.alaskapublic.org/2018/03/05/mixing-science-with-traditional -knowledge-researchers-hope-to-get-seal-oil-on-menu/.

2. David Bornstein, "From Many Corners, Journalism Seeking Solutions," *The New York Times* (December 13, 2016), https://www.nytimes .com/2016/12/13/opinion/from-many-corners-journalism-seeking -solutions.html.

3. Jim Rutenberg, "A 'Dewey Defeats Truman' Lesson for the Digital Age," *New York Times* (November 9, 2016), https://www.nytimes.com /2016/11/09/business/media/media-trump-clinton.html.

4. Sara Jerving, Kate Jennings, Masako Hirsch, and Susanne Rust, "What Exxon Knew about the Earth's Melting Arctic," *Los Angeles Times* (October 9, 2015), http://graphics.latimes.com/exxon-arctic.

5. Erica Martinson, "Melting Alaska May Not Accelerate Climate Change as Expected, Scientists Now Say," *Alaska Dispatch News* (July 8, 2016), https://www.adn.com/alaska-news/environment/2016/06/01/melting -alaska-may-not-accelerate-climate-change-as-expected-scientists -now-say.

6. Bethany Davies, "Climate Change," Antartic Glaciers (September 25, 2014), http://www.antarcticglaciers.org/glaciers-and-climate /climate-change.

7. Lara Setrakian, "3 Ways to Fix a Broken News Industry," TED Talk (January 2017), https://www.ted.com/talks /lara_setrakian_3_ways_to_fix_a_broken_news_industry.

8. Jurriaan Kamp (ed.), *Ode for Intelligent Optimists* 8, no. 2 (2011).

9. Marco Visscher, "A Politically Incorrect Solution to Climate Change," *Ode for Intelligent Optimists* 8, no. 2 (2011): 46.

10. Daniel Ben-Ami, "Growth is Good," *Ode for Intelligent Optimists* 8, no. 2 (2011): 44.

11. Rene Bogaarts and Marco Visscher, with Gerbert van der Aa, "Wish You Were Here," *Ode for Intelligent Optimists* 8, no. 2 (2011).

12. Elizabeth Rosenthal, "New Jungles Prompt a Debate on Rain Forests," *New York Times* (January 29, 2009), http://www.nytimes.com/2009/01/30 /science/earth/30forest.html.

13. *Alaska Journal of Commerce*, October 25, 2012, http://www.alaska journal.com/issues/2012-10-25/alaska-journal-commerce-october -issue-4-2012#.WRHmDFPyuQO.

14. Bjoern H. Amland and George Jahn, "Norway's Oil Finds Shield It from Economic Gloom," *Huffington Post* (August 30, 2011), http://www .huffingtonpost.com/huff-wires/20110830/eu-norway-oil-riches.

CHAPTER 15

1. Bill Clinton, "President Bill Clinton's Address to 2016 LMU Undergradutates," Loyola Marymount University, Los Angeles, CA, http:// lmu.edu/archives/commencement2016/videosandspeeches /presidentbillclintonsaddressto2016lmuundergraduates/.

2. wpcomimportuser1, "Talking to Arthur Laffer About Taxes, Taxes, Taxes and Barack Obama," *Time* (December 7, 2007), http://business.time .com/2007/12/07/talking_to_arthur_laffer_about/.

3. Max Ehrenfreund, "How Hillary Clinton's Positions Have Changed as She's Run Against Bernie Sanders," *Washington Post* (April 29, 2016), https://www.washingtonpost.com/news/wonk/wp/2016/04/29/how -hillary-clintons-positions-have-changed-while-running-against-bernie -sanders/?utm_term=.143a5ef81d50.

4. Larry J. Sabato, *The Kennedy Half-Century: The Presidency, Assassination, and Lasting Legacy of John F. Kennedy* (Bloomsbury, 2013).

5. Darren Goode, "Wyden, Murkowski Team on Energy," Politico (November 19, 2012), http://www.politico.com/story/2012/11 /wyden-murkowski-ready-for-energy-partnership-084019.

CHAPTER 16

1. Guy Norris, "Lockheed Pairs Commercial Herc and Cargo Airship," *Aviation Week* (July 14, 2016), http://aviationweek.com/shownews /lockheed-pairs-commercial-herc-and-cargo-airship.

2. With Jim Eber (Entrepreneur Press, 2015).

3. California State University, Chico, Department of Mechanical and Mechatronic Engineering and Sustainable Manufacturing, "BS Sustainable Manufacturing," USC Chico (2016), http://www.csuchico .edu/mmem/programs/bsmanufacturing_technology/index.shtml.

4. Jessica Torres, "Understanding the Biotech Market in Brazil," *BIOtechNOW* (May 27, 2014), http://www.biotech-now.org/events/2014/05 /understanding-the-biotech-market-in-brazil.

5. Barry Eichengreen, *The European Economy since 1945: Coordinated Capitalism and Beyond* (Princeton University Press, 2008).

6. Cassie Werber, "It's Taken 25 Years, but the 'Happiness Gap' between Post-Soviet Countries and Their Peers Has Finally Closed," Quartz (November 7, 2016), http://qz.com/829339/its-taken-25-years-but-the-happiness -gap-between-post-soviet-countries-and-their-peers-has-finally-closed.

7. Ernst and Young, *Hitting the Sweet Spot: The Growth of the Middle Class in Emerging Markets* (Ernst and Young, 2013).

8. Greenleaf Book Group, 2014.

9. Eric Thayer, "Is Organic Food Passé? New Food Producer Says 'Post Organic' Is the Future," *Christian Science Monitor* (February 2017), http:// www.csmonitor.com/Business/The-Bite/2017/0223/Is-organic -food-passe-New-food-producer-says-post-organic-is-the-future.

About the Author

DAVID PARISH has spent the past three decades as an independent business and nonprofit consultant, lobbyist, entrepreneur, and author. During that time, he has worked among global energy and mining industry leaders, giving him a bird's-eye view of natural resource development in the 21st century. David has also advocated for efforts to address autism and developmental disability challenges, teen suicide, child abuse prevention, youth tobacco and marijuana prevention, and funding for public broadcasting. In these endeavors, he has worked with elected officials—from governors to legislators of all political persuasions—as well as environmental activists and Native leaders.

David founded a global consulting practice advising dozens of companies doing business in Russia on political, regulatory, and healthcare issues and was publisher of the *Pacific Russia Oil & Gas Report.*

His client and volunteer experience reflects a deep belief that a robust economy with strong environmental stewardship is critical to providing the resources necessary to support healthy communities. An active outdoor enthusiast, David is a tireless advocate who has served on numerous community boards spearheading programs for children, especially those improving parks and recreational opportunities.

With Alaska as his home base for a diverse set of local, national, and international clients, David has worked around the globe as a business consultant and advisor, service volunteer, and curious traveler interested in how the traditional divides of "us-versus-them" approaches to natural resource development can be bridged and how the wealth from responsible natural resource development can be a catalyst for better environmental stewardship and the elimination of poverty.